Passing the Torch
Transfer Strategies for Your Family Business

Mike Cohn

LIBERTY HALL
PRESS™

LIBERTY HALL PRESS books are published by LIBERTY HALL PRESS, a division of TAB BOOKS Inc. Its trademark, consisting of the words "LIBERTY HALL PRESS" and the portrayal of Benjamin Franklin, is registered in the United States Patent and Trademark Office.

First Edition
First Printing

©1990 by TAB BOOKS Inc.
Printed in the United States of America

Library of Congress Cataloging-in-Publication Data

Cohn, Mike
Passing the torch : transfer strategies for your family business /
by Mike Cohn.
p. cm.
ISBN 0-8306-3050-3
1. Family corporations—United States—Popular works. 2. Business enterprises—Registration and transfer—United States—Popular works. 3. Tax planning—United States. I. Title.
KF1466.Z9C6 1989
346.73'0668—dc20
[347.306668]   89-13259
                                                         CIP

TAB BOOKS Inc. offers software for sale.
For information and a catalog, please contact:

TAB Software Department
Blue Ridge Summit, PA 17294-0850

Questions regarding the content of this book
should be addressed to:

Reader Inquiry Branch
TAB BOOKS Inc.
Blue Ridge Summit, PA 17294-0214

Vice President & Editorial Director: David J. Conti
Book Editor: Joanne M. Slike
Production: Katherine Brown
Book Design: Jaclyn B. Saunders

Contents

Acknowledgments

SPECIAL THANKS TO CHERRIL FOR HER PATIENCE AND ENCOURAGEMENT during the constant chaos that accompanied this book. Thanks to my sister, Jane Mollenkamp, for her editorial comments and revisions.

I'm especially grateful to my wife, Jan, for her critical support, her perspective, and her creativity—and to my family for giving me the experience of growing up in a family business—and the love for it.

Finally, thanks to the people at The Cohn Financial Group who helped me in this book's preparation, and all of its clients for providing me with the experiences and ideas that are the foundation for this book.

Introduction

Protecting the "Golden Goose"

YOU ARE A BUSINESS OWNER AND HAVE REACHED THE STAGE IN YOUR LIFE WHEN you are thinking about your retirement and the orderly transition of your family business. Maybe you will sell the business, or perhaps you will transfer the ownership to a competent family member or key employee. You have worked hard for decades to see your company prosper and grow, and now your mind is filled with questions on how best to protect "the golden goose" that has supported your family and employees for so many years.

Now it is up to the next generation, your son or daughter or key person, to build the business further. What qualities of leadership and business acumen must your successor possess in order to ensure the survival and profitability of your business? What strategies should you use to be certain of a smooth transition of ownership? What are the choices that you must make now in order to promote succession of leadership that will leave your company running in the black perhaps for several generations to come?

These are the questions that I will deal with in this book. And the answers will not only involve numbers or clearly definable business terminology; the human and emotional issues of business transfer are of paramount importance in making the right decisions. What you are contemplating is a major life change, fraught with financial and emotional risks. My goal in this book is to reduce your anxiety by carefully mapping out the territory that you must cover in order to make informed, calculated decisions based on facts.

At this time you may not even know what decisions you need to make. I promise you, however, that if you take it step by step, following my guidelines and advice, by the time you finish reading this book your strategy for successful business transition will become apparent to you, and your decisions will be much less difficult to make and to implement.

I will show you exactly how to take stock of where you are, pinpoint where you are going with your business and retirement plans, and plan precisely how to get there.

This book will:

- Highlight and discuss most of the issues and potential conflicts that will arise out of your current "life cycle."

- Detail a strategy for you to cope successfully with the relevant issues concerning family business transfer of ownership and control.

- Help you to anticipate contingencies and problems that might arise out of your decision.

- Show you how to avoid unnecessary taxation on transferring the business so that you keep more of the wealth you've created.

- Show you exactly what to look for and what to avoid in planning your next business move.

- Help you develop a transfer strategy that suits your needs and goals.

It is my experience that many business owners, although superb at implementing their own decisions, are often unable to communicate clearly with their family and employees concerning important business plans and ideas. Although your situation may be unusual or even totally unique to you, there are numerous issues that you share with other business owners. I will identify these issues for you and show you how to deal with them most effectively.

You will learn in Part I, "Seven Personal Hurdles to a Successful Business Transfer," how to resolve the conflicts that are common to all owner-managers of family businesses. There are millions of business people who have already gone through the experiences that you are now having. I will discuss those experiences in the light of your current life situation. I will help you understand and formulate realistic and effective goals, and appreciate what your own "risk tolerance" level is. Family business transition can be a very confusing and complex period in your life, emotionally as well as financially. But there are guidelines to follow that will ease your transition and maximize the financial independence and security you deserve.

Some of the variables are under your control, and some are not. I will also show you what your alternative solution may be, and how to determine exactly what plan is right for you, taking into account the complexities of family psychology, staff psychology, and the emotional issues that accompany relinquishing control.

In Part II, "Transfer Strategies for Your Business," I will outline various transfer strategies that my company has used successfully in hundreds of business and family situations throughout the United States. In this section I will detail techniques that you most likely have never considered, and I will show you exactly how to apply these techniques and strategies to your particular situation.

Successfully implementing a business transfer strategy requires creativity, flexibility, and above all *commitment*. Effective transfer strategies are based on where you are *now* in your business and family life. I will show you exactly how each strategy can be set up so that if conditions change at any time, your plan may be altered and even abandoned depending on your specific contingencies.

It is important, however, to realize that there are some "points of no return." I will show you how to prepare your plan so that you will not have to take any unnecessary risks or cross that juncture until you are prepared and all the players and proper conditions are in place. Up to the point of no turning back, you will learn how to implement an "abort" plan to change the players, timing, or the whole structure of your succession plan.

If you have done the proper planning and are prepared, then after the no-turning-back point, you will undoubtedly experience a sense of euphoria—of control and confidence that you are doing the right thing to protect your business, your family, and your future. (I have heard many exclamations of delight and relief at this point in the plan, such as "I feel a tremendous burden has been lifted off my shoulders.") Good planning and informed decisions are your best insurance for peace of mind.

In Part II, I will discuss, in depth, formulas for determining your company's value, and how to maximize that value in various ways. You could create a new corporation, or sell your business to a key man or outside third party. These various strategies have been researched and tested thoroughly, and I will guide you through the details as they apply to your particular situation.

You will have to consider a wide variety of input in making your succession plans. Suppose your spouse wants to run the business after your death or encourages you to divide up the estate equally—yet you know the outcome of such a plan would prohibit the chances of your business surviving. Some key people have been employed by you for 20 or 30 years and play a large part in the success of your business. These are your "adopted family members," and you will want to consider their roles and futures carefully in structuring an equitable and effective plan, especially if they are expected to work for your spouse, son, or daughter.

Your key person who has devoted 15 or 20 years to making your business more profitable may be much more deserving than your son or daughter who might complicate the business and possibly destroy it with bickering and greed. You must think carefully about the key players in your plan; maybe your son would make a wonderful president of your company in a few years, and you want to protect his succession interest in the firm. Perhaps you have in-laws who are competent and wish to join your firm as managers. There are ways to accomplish your goals without endangering either the future of your company or the security of any deserving employees.

I will reveal to you in this book my experiences concerning how to determine who is ready to handle the business responsibilities of running a company. I will also show you exactly how careful estate planning will guarantee security to your spouse in the event of your death without requiring the spouse to run the business.

In Part III, you will learn how recent legislation may require you to change your estate planning. More importantly, you will learn how estate planning and business transfer planning can be coordinated to keep the family together and reduce estate taxation for your heirs.

You are not alone. It is unnecessary for you to attempt to resolve or even delineate the problems that you must face in creating an effective, realistic succession plan. In *Passing the Torch: Transfer Strategies for Your Family Business,* I will introduce you to other business and family people who have successfully gone through the same transition that you are now contemplating. With their experience and my guidance, I hope that by the time you have finished reading this book your anxieties concerning ''passing the torch'' will be vastly diminished. I hope that as you begin developing your own game plan, you will face the challenge with optimism, excitement, and confidence. If this book provides new insights, guides you through difficult obstacles, and creates a vision of positive alternatives for you, then it will have accomplished its purpose.

Part I
Overcoming the Seven Personal Hurdles to a Successful Business Transfer

1

The American Dream Machine

THE SUCCESS STORY THAT OFTEN ACCOMPANIES THE FOUNDER OF A FAMILY business has all the makings of a modern epic. The founder struggles and perseveres in the face of overwhelming odds. In so doing, he or she becomes a hero in a world that needs heroes, a central figure who inspires others, and the catalyst for family ideals and traditions. As a result of the founder's vision, leadership, and bravery, the family achieves economic prosperity; the founder gains power and recognition; and the community is enriched through the creation of jobs. Ideally, the epic would end and stories would be written about the hero's accomplishments.

Reality, however, is usually quite different. At the height of the business founder's success and power, someone comes along—a family member, trusted advisor, or even an employee—and suggests that the founder relinquish the reins of the business to others.

At this point, the epic frequently becomes a tragedy. The founder doesn't want to relinquish his power and the business becomes fragmented as those involved choose sides. As the hero becomes defensive, power is consolidated and battles begin. Often the tragedy ends as the hero, having lost his power base, is vanquished and shrunken in stature.

I grew up in a family-owned business that had been started by my great-grandfather in 1873. The business began as a general merchandise store and evolved over time into the retail sales of men's, women's, and children's clothing. When my grandfather died in 1944, my dad took over the business with my mom's cousin. Dad bought the cousin out in 1955, and I don't think they've talked to each other since.

I began working in my dad's business when I was six years old by helping to assemble paper boxes, run errands, and ride in the van that delivered packages to customers. Our entire family revolved around the business: My mom worked there, and my sister worked there on holidays and in between school vacations. More importantly, all the meals at home were planned around when Dad was coming home from "the store." We'd always wait for Dad to come home before we had lunch and supper.

The store was the subject of most family discussions. My dad would hire friends to work in the store during the Christmas holidays—wrapping packages, making deliveries, working on "the floor" to make sales. The store was a source of pride for me and a source of revenue for friends. The business grew as Dad expanded it to additional locations. Everything seemed in order.

As I grew older, Dad became increasingly resistant to change. For a clothing store to succeed, it has to stay current with fads and fashions and provide the latest "look" to the consumer. Not my dad. When neckties narrowed and suit lapels widened, Dad steadfastly believed that wide ties and narrow lapels would come back. And they did, but not fast enough.

In 1967, while I was in college, Dad closed the store; he didn't sell it, he liquidated it—the worst of all possible conclusions to a family business. During a liquidation, there is no value paid for goodwill, no value given for reputation or commitment to community. People buy assets for pennies on the dollar. And finally, when there are only a few pieces left, a liquidator arrives, loads it all onto his truck, and carts it away. What's left is an empty building. And sometimes, an empty family.

When the store closed, a large part of our family heritage was lost. For more than three generations the store had been the primary focus of the family's activities. All of a sudden, the store wasn't there anymore. Years later, I understood the dynamics that drove my father's business decisions.

HUMANISTIC PSYCHOLOGY AND BUSINESS TRANSFERS

When I went to college, I pursued psychology and ultimately earned a Masters Degree in a unique discipline known as humanistic psychology. Abraham Maslow, the father of humanistic psychology, explored human motivations and concluded that our inner nature, our basic human capacities, are generally "good." Our basic needs for safety and security, for belongingness and affection, for respect and self-respect, and for self-actualization are what motivate all of us. Destructiveness, sadism, cruelty, and so on are our reactions to frustrations experienced when our basic needs cannot be realized (actualized). Maslow concluded that when we encourage our inner nature to guide our lives, we become healthy, productive, and happy. The tenets of humanistic psychology—security, growth in the human experience, and reasons underlying decision-making—are instructive for family business systems.

Most tax experts—whether they are accountants, attorneys, or financial professionals—consider and utilize the technical aspects of financial planning. That is, how do we minimize corporate or personal income or estate taxes? How do we plan for the transfer of the business in a tax-efficient manner? How do we pass the assets of the estate through to the next generation so as to minimize unnecessary transfer taxes? Technical considerations are significant and certainly important in the financial planning process. Yet the humanistic issues cannot be ignored: the client's needs, desires, fears, wants, and goals are as crucial to financial planning as tax and investment codes. To ignore these humanistic issues is to ignore basic needs—for safety and security, belongingness and affection, respect and self-respect, and self-actualization. It is this needs-based, client-centered approach, coupled with extensive technical skills, that form the foundation for my company, and the thesis for this book on business transfer planning.

We've identified a number of reasons, which are explored further in Chapters 2 through 10, why business owners are reluctant to "pass the torch." By understanding and addressing these issues, you are in a position to apply the practical solutions that make up the remainder of this book.

The problems inherent in a business transfer cannot be oversimplified. The emotional and psychological trauma that accompanies the transfer of a family business will cause even the strongest business owner to pause. Has he made the right decision? Should he take an easier way out and sell to a large conglomerate?

Maslow understood this trauma in his hierarchy of needs. Growth toward higher levels of accomplishment causes many people to walk away from the challenge. Business owners succeed against overwhelming odds, and the challenge of transferring the family business cannot be considered lightly. But the rewards, if understood in the context of human growth, can be the greatest accomplishment of all.

"Passing the torch" may be a true act of self-realization and self-actualization. As the business owner evolves from hero to mere mortal, there is an opportunity for gaining wisdom. A business transfer does not have to be tantamount to loss of stature in the family and the community.

THE LAST FRONTIER

The family-owned business is one of the last frontiers in which the American Dream can be realized. Just as the American pioneer discovered new lands, the American entrepreneur has created new products, new services, and new technologies that have had profound changes on our daily lives.

Families have grown up as entrepreneurs' visions became reality. As jobs are created, communities have developed, been influenced by, and influenced the business and its owners.

Although entrepreneurs will always be a part of our society's fabric, an increasing number of business owners—those who started their businesses after World War II—are approaching retirement. Anticipation of leisure time and activities is generally overshadowed by unresolved business ownership and transfer issues.

As the founder/owner ages or dies, the vision that drove the business fades or dies with him. Seventy percent of family businesses do not survive into the second generation. Businesses are sold, merged, or liquidated.

When the vision is lost, business purpose is lost. Vision motivates people to take risk, to grow and change, to imagine something better and work toward those goals. Business owners without purpose or direction will ultimately fail.

The health and welfare of a family business have a pervasive influence that extends far beyond the business's physical facilities. All family members are affected by the business owner's success or failure, or how brightly the spark of commitment glows and in whom it glows. Ultimately, anyone associated with the family business is affected: suppliers, customers, employees, and the community-at-large.

Changes in a family business have far-reaching consequences. Imagine standing on the bank of a quiet pond and throwing a pebble into the water. The ripples on the surface of the water extend outward and cover the entire pond. Making decisions regarding change in ownership and control of the family business is like tossing that pebble into the water.

Family businesses permeate our economy. When a family business ceases to exist—either because it is sold or because it is liquidated—we are all affected. Family businesses make up 90 percent of the 15 million businesses in the U.S. One-third of the *Fortune* 500 are either family owned or family controlled. Family businesses account for 40 percent of our gross national product; yet, the typical family business has a life expectancy of only 24 years. Incredibly then, every 24 years, over 10 million businesses will need to be created and survive just to *replace* the goods and services from the 70 percent who do not survive. In other words, we will have to run harder and harder just to stay in the same place.

For every two family businesses that continue into the second generation, four do not. Of those two that succeed, only one of those survives into a third generation.

THE TRAGEDY OF BUSINESS FAILURE

Families frequently encounter problems during the process of transferring the family business. Usually these problems can be resolved. At other times, business transfer problems result in tragic outcomes, including:

- Qualified family members who become disenfranchised because they never have an opportunity to continue the family business.
- Ill-prepared children and employees for a leadership role.
- The owner who is unaware of the options available.
- The owner who is unwilling to relinquish control.
- The family who suffers extreme financial loss, not because of taxation, but rather through lack of planning.

For the past 13 years, I've worked with hundreds of diverse business owners: some started their business, others married into it; some received the business as a gift, others inherited it; some bought the business in a friendly purchase and others bought it as the solution to a conflict. All of these clients shared one thing. They are all successful business people. And because they chose effective, although sometimes quite different, business transfer strategies, their businesses remain successful. This book is about perpetuation, "preservation from oblivion." Throughout these pages, we will explore the perpetuation of business, of wealth, of jobs, and of family.

Your first challenge is to pick up the pebble as you stand alongside the pond. If you are like most business owners, your business represents most of your personal wealth—and most of the years of your life. Whether you sell the business outright, transfer it within the family, or transfer it to key employees, you will be faced with many soul-searching decisions. The decisions you make should attempt to balance your responsibilities to yourself, your family, your employees, and, most importantly, your business.

Your challenge, then, is not to repeat the failures of others, but to learn from them. The next American Dream could be the successful perpetuation of the family business.

2

Factors that Ruin
a Family Business

IN THE NEXT FEW CHAPTERS, WE WILL DISCUSS SEVEN PSYCHOLOGICAL AND emotional conflicts, barriers, traumas, and needs that generally arise when you begin to think about passing the torch. Any one of these can wreck your transfer plans; once aware of these issues, you will be better prepared for some of the challenges you will face.

Some of these issues may appear as personal obstacles to overcome. They may require from you, and others, a special level of understanding and greater awareness of your family relationships. Others require ongoing communication with family members and successors.

You will overcome a major hurdle after you resolve these seven issues. Then you will be able to focus objectively on the transfer strategies discussed in Part II. How you resolve these issues has a major impact on how the transfer should be structured.

Attorneys, accountants, and financial advisors often focus exclusively on the tax and legal aspects of transfer strategies. They seldom address the underlying emotional and psychological issues that are involved. By addressing those issues first, we strive to defuse emotionally intense situations, and address important family issues. Only *after* those are resolved do we focus on the transfer strategies: the technical, legal, or tax aspects. This approach sets the stage for a successful transfer.

1. **Lack of clear goals or objectives.** When the business owner lacks clear goals or objectives, there is a confusion of purpose, insecurity on the part of successors, and no definite time to accomplish results.
2. **Conflict between the business and family "system."** When the business and family "system" overlap, the rules from one system may conflict with the rules of the other. Sometimes this is the result of a lack of communication. Addressing difficult issues now as you explore transferring your business will allow you to determine if the potential family conflicts can be resolved. If not, you can begin to make alternative plans. Pushing potential problems under the rug will only cause them to be larger in the future.
3. **Life cycle "out of sync."** As we age, we pass through different stages of life, with each stage having its own particular characteristics. Our thinking is influenced by the particular stage of our life cycle and our business decisions reflect our present stage of life. When people at different life stages discuss their business objectives and goals, the differences in values, style, and attitude may lead to conflict in the business. Understanding the impact that life cycles have on business decisions is a critical part of developing a transfer plan. This allows all parties to appreciate the biological and psychological changes that other family members are experiencing.
4. **Lack of commitment (yours and others).** Commitment to the success of the successors and their commitment to you is an essential ingredient to passing the torch. A commitment allows a free flow of communication, a sharing and an understanding of values. Without it, the effort may never get off the ground.
5. **Not letting go (of control).** Not letting go is often the result of not having anything to "go toward." Holding on to what one has may be safer than letting go, especially when there are no positive alternatives in sight. Understanding the emotional trauma that accompanies the owner's letting go is important in order for all family members to prevent a major problem from developing.
6. **Financial dependence on the business.** Are you financially independent of the business? Or do you rely on the business to provide for your financial well-being? Understanding the amount of your financial dependence will help you structure a successful transfer strategy.
7. **Overlooking the impact that key employees have.** What impact will key employees have on your transfer plans? Overlooking their importance can jeopardize the success of your efforts since their cooperation is often critical during the transition from one generation to the next.

Now, let's explore these seven issues in detail in the following chapters.

3

Establishing
Clear Goals

LEONARD'S BUSINESS HAS BEEN IN THE FAMILY FOR NEARLY 100 YEARS. HE
feels fortunate he has two capable sons in management right now who can take
over the business for another generation.

Recently, several businesses like Leonard's sold out to large chains. In talking with his peers, Leonard realized he might receive $3 to $4 million cash if he
sold the business. A quick calculation revealed that the interest alone on $3 to $4
million would far surpass the annual salary Leonard draws from his business.

Leonard looks at the portraits of his father, grandfather and great grandfa-
thers on his office wall and wonders what they would say right now.

* * * *

Someday you may find yourself in Leonard's situation. You may be approached by a large company that is interested in acquiring your business. They
have significant dollars to offer, as well as employment agreements and a variety
of other compensation packages. The ''deal'' may give you financial freedom
beyond your wildest dreams.

Is this the best avenue for you? For your family? For your business? What
other factors, if any, should you investigate? This chapter will explore these considerations.

Throughout the U.S., most industries are dominated by independently
owned firms. Some of these firms are family owned, some are owned by shareholders who are unrelated, and some are owned by partners. The generally

11

accepted definition of an independently owned firm is one in which decisions are made by owners who are active in the business at a local level. Although "an independent firm" may have branches or operations throughout the U.S. with a home office physically removed from the various places where business is conducted, one important fact remains: decisions are made by a core group of individuals who are either related as family members or related through a commonality of business interests.

Most buy-sell, stock purchase, or partnership agreements define what happens when the owners or principals die or become disabled. What happens when the owners want to dispose of their interests while they are still alive? What will happen to the business, the family, the employees? Should the business be transferred to family members, to key employees, or sold to an outside third party? Complex issues must be resolved before you formulate your decision.

SHOULD YOU REMAIN INDEPENDENT?

One of the first questions to ask yourself is whether or not you want the business to stay in the family, or to remain independent. Why? The independent, family-owned firm is owned by one or more family members; decision-making is controlled by the local owners. Compare this to being a subsidiary or division of a larger company in which decisions are made by executives in a corporate home office located elsewhere. Do you even know who will be your successors? Are they ready? When will they be ready? Can they afford it? You will need to clearly understand the advantages of remaining as an independent firm and you will need to communicate these advantages to the next generation. The next generation needs to be as excited about opportunities and as committed to the business as you.

If there are no family members to succeed you, then consider your key employees as potential "buyers." Even if you don't think they have the financial resources to buy the business, don't count them out. (We will explore strategies for key employee business transfers in Part II.)

Why should the family firm remain independent? Take a few minutes before reading further, and outline on Form 3-1 the advantages of a family-owned business.

A 1986 survey asked business owners their reasons for passing on the family business. The answers may be helpful to you in completing the outline:

34% Opportunity for children.
  • Provides freedom, control of their personal destiny, and autonomy;
  • Provides opportunity for personal growth, creativity, and expression.

Form 3-1

Why Keep the Family Business in The Family?

1. _____

   _____

2. _____

   _____

3. _____

   _____

4. _____

   _____

5. _____

   _____

21% Perpetuate heritage.
- Builds tradition, history, and roots.
- Creates living memorial.

15% Keep family together.
- Helps family work together;
- Strengthens family bond;
- Allows more family time together.

10% Generate financial advantages and wealth.

8% Ensures own retirement and personal purpose past age 65.

(Continued)

6%   Protects loyal employees.

5%   Provides family with financial security.

1%   Benefits society.

Overall, the survey concluded there was a belief that the family business benefits the family. Offspring have greater opportunities for freedom and growth, and family traditions and the business heritage are maintained and enriched.[1]

If you identified positive reasons for keeping the family business independent, or agreed with the preceding survey results, then like me, you must wonder why an incredible number of family business transfers fail.

TIME: HOW MUCH DO YOU HAVE?

The process of preparing yourself and your business for a transfer may begin three to five years prior to the actual transfer. Or, it may be only three to five months.

Why begin so early? Because if you plan to transfer your business in three years, there are only 750 working days left to put your house in order. Once you have made the decision to consider transferring your business ownership, there is much to do.

The longer the lead time, the greater the financial alternatives available to you, and the smaller the risk for the successors. A short lead time (six months) usually means the transaction will be financed out of future earnings of the company. If the business isn't successful in the future, the earnings to pay you may not be available. A longer lead time allows you more time to set corporate funds aside, thus guaranteeing your payments at a later date. (Part II addresses this in more detail.)

ARE YOUR GOALS ON A COLLISION COURSE?

Perhaps your goals for the business are to husband the assets so the assets can be used to buy you out. Simultaneously, you may find that the successors plan to use the business assets to expand and grow. Such a potential conflict should be discussed and resolved prior to the actual business transfer.

One client found himself as the target of a minority shareholder suit led by his son. The client had been gifting stock to his children, with the intent of using corporate assets to provide a salary continuation agreement for himself at his retirement, in lieu of keeping the stock and having the business buy it back. The son, who had other plans for the corporate hoard, threatened to sue. Ultimately the family chose sides. It took years to finally resolve the issues.

What about personal goals? If you are planning to grow and expand your business, while simultaneously spending winter months in warmer climates, someone has to care for the business. Are your business goals shared by others or are they unilateral objectives?

Achieving goals is a team effort, whether in a business or in a family. Communication is important to receive support from all those who will help you accomplish your goals.

OTHER CONSIDERATIONS

Other considerations important to your decision will be based on the quality of your product or service, the loyalty of your employees, the expectations of your customers, your reputation in the market, your suppliers, and your peers and associates who own other businesses within your industry.

Will the quality of your business product or service be maintained or enhanced by remaining a family business? Will the next generation understand and appreciate the loyalty of your key employees? Will you develop a competitive edge by ''keeping'' the business in the family as opposed to selling it? Will your supplier relationships be maintained or changed? What are your suppliers doing to perpetuate their own businesses?

Finally, and importantly, are your peers and associates selling out to third parties or transferring their businesses to children or employees? This may be the greatest influence on your decision. If someone sells to a conglomerate and has only horror stories to describe the relationship, your commitment to working with family members may be greatly enhanced. On the other hand, if the sale was good for the owner, the business, and the employees, you may be influenced to do the same.

SUMMARY

You may feel like Alice in Wonderland when she asked the Cheshire Cat, ''Would you tell me, please, which way I ought to go from here?'' The Cheshire Cat answered, ''That depends a good deal on where you want to get to. If you don't care, then it doesn't matter which way you go.'' In the family business, if you don't know where *you're* going, then the overwhelming odds are that your business will not survive you. Your first step is to set goals, objectives, and a time frame in which to achieve them.

Solving Family Conflicts

TO MAXIMIZE THE SUCCESS OF A BUSINESS TRANSFER TO FAMILY MEMBERS or employees or to enhance your value if you plan to sell to a third party, you should begin to plan three to five years in advance of the target date. The longer the lead time, the greater will be your rewards. If you wait until you are ready to get out, let go, or retire, you may not have as much flexibility in structuring the transaction.

A three- to five-year lead time offers an opportunity to test people in different roles and evaluate their maturity, commitment, business acumen, and leadership. If you know who your successors will be, this lead time will allow you to work with the next generation of owner-managers, prepare them for a greater degree of readiness, and set up a jointly agreed upon timetable for the transfer to occur.

Latent conflicts may emerge during this advance-planning phase as you begin to evaluate the potential successors and heirs. If they fail to meet your expectations, you may decide that a sale to an outside third party is a viable alternative. Prior to this advance planning, everything ran smoothly—since no one, least of all you, questioned your authority. As soon as you enter this phase, you become more critical of your potential successors. Now as you evaluate employees' performances, and even family relationships, you do so with a different eye.

When you begin to consider the transfer or perpetuation of the family business, it is common, at the same time, to consider the impact that process will have on the business family. According to a study described in *The Family in Business* by Paul Rosenblatt and his associates, 90% of the families studied reported tension or stress in family relationships as a result of the family business.[1]

WHERE CONFLICT BEGINS

If you have family members in your business, it is likely that certain rules they learned in the family as a child have carried over into the business. These rules may guide their day-to-day behavior. You may never have made a clear distinction when they entered the business that the business's rules and family rules differ. What is appropriate or tolerated at home may be inappropriate and cannot be allowed in the business environment. Understanding these differences is important in heading off potential conflicts that may be hidden beneath the surface of relationships.

Children growing up in families learn to abide by various rules within the family system. Those rules protect the children. They teach them how to survive in the world and give them a measure of security as they grow older. They learn to operate outside of the family system and on their own. If children go to work in another unrelated business, they will, in all likelihood, be trained in their job, as well as told the rules and procedures of the business. When they come to work in the family firm, they may not understand the philosophical differences between the business and family.

For example, Rosenblatt found that one source of tension was over financial resources. Conservative financial management in the company may create profits and wealth that are shared with family members. The family members may not fully understand or appreciate the hard work required to create the wealth. Family members may benefit from the hard work, perhaps without working hard themselves. When those family members enter the business, their attitude toward spending business dollars may be the same attitude they had toward family dollars. The younger family members may want to expand the business—new ideas, new acquisitions, new ventures—without fully understanding the importance of the dollars they are putting at risk.

On the other hand, well-thought-out expansion and growth plans should not be ignored by the older generation. Growth and progress are essential to the business's survival.

CONFLICT BETWEEN BUSINESS AND FAMILY

Understanding the business and the family as interrelated systems offers insight into some important aspects of a family business transfer. Why? Because even as the business and the family exist as independent systems, the two systems inevitably overlap. The success or failure of the business transfer often begins (and unfortunately ends) in the overlap—the area where business and family become intertwined. It is in this overlap that conflict can occur.

As Paul Rosenblatt writes, "Often the two systems compete for the time, energy, and financial resources of individual family members and of the family collectively. The goals of the two systems inevitably clash some of the time. The competition for the resources and clash of goals can create problems, and the ways family members deal with that competition and clash can also create problems."[2]

When the systems overlap, conflict occurs because the rules of the family system contradict the rules of the business system (or vice versa). The result is strain on both systems. (See Fig. 4-1.)

Ivan Lansberg, a Yale professor who studies family businesses, found that conflict occurs because of the differences innate in the family and the organizational "purpose": The family's purpose is to care for and nurture family members; the business's purpose is to provide goods and services at a profit.[3]

Fig. 4-1. System overlap.

Family Purpose	Business Purpose
Decision Making Parent is vested with authority (may not be the Business Boss)	*Decision Making* The Boss or CEO (may be different from family decision maker)
Participation Birth precludes rational hiring policy	*Participation* Hire participants based on competence, experience
Money Participants receive allowances based on "need"	*Money* Participants receive income and benefits based on performance and skill required
Training Provide learning opportunities designed to satisfy individual needs	*Training* Provide learning opportunities designed to satisfy business needs
Review Regard participants as "ends" rather than "means." Encourage growth and expression	*Review* Regard participants as "means" rather than "ends. Encourage growth consistent with organizational purpose
Recognition No differentiation among participants	*Recognition* Recognize and reward high performers

Conflict occurs when rules of the two systems collide

The six areas of operation highlighted in Fig. 4-1 have different rules regarding participation, compensation arrangements, appraisal of activities, and training given to members of the particular system. For example, when family members are given tasks and responsibilities in the family, the objective is to develop the individual, instill positive values, and nurture personal growth. Tasks and responsibilities in the business serve a business function and may do little in the way of promoting individual growth. If a family member is given a position of responsibility in the business without understanding this fundamental difference, stress occurs individually and system-wide. Efficiency in the business is reduced, while stress on all the participants is increased.

One business owner spoiled his children as they grew up. He continued to bail them out when they encountered financial difficulties. The older son, at about age 25, started several business ventures, all of which were financial disasters. Dad rescued him each time. Years later, as it came time for Dad to seek a business successor, he mentally disqualified the older son as a candidate because of his fiscal irresponsibility in the past. Although by that time the son had matured and was active in the family business (as sales manager), Dad elected to sell to an outside third party. The family rules (take care of the family members), which guided the family's direction, did not fit the business rules. The owner neglected to explain to family participants that the game was different. The son struck out before he had a chance to learn the rules and play.

Paul Rosenblatt states: "The key to managing the family business is to recognize the separateness of the two systems and the difference in goals . . . if that difference is fully appreciated, management does not become simple in a family business, but it becomes in some sense more sane."[4]

John Ward (*Keeping the Family Business Healthy*) writes, "The process of resolving these conflicts must be established long before the children arrive in the business. It must begin in the home: in the lessons children are taught, in the way the family conducts itself. It continues with . . . the children's entry into the business and their preparation for leadership roles . . . . Families find that considering these challenges ahead of time increases the chances of solving them to everyone's satisfaction."[5]

IN-LAWS AND OUTLAWS

Conflict in the family business is usually more intense than in other relationships because the conflict spills over into personal lives, weekends, holidays, and family outings, and affects children as well as grandchildren. Staying away from the family gatherings only makes the situation worse, since the rest of the family often talks about those who are absent. Attending family events can be equally as unpleasant.

Life-cycle issues become confused when the "adult" in business is still viewed by his parents as a child in the family setting. Brothers who are business partners may still relate to each other as they did when they were 10 years old.

Spouses may never feel "part of the family," and in retaliation, may enthusiastically join the "outsiders" group, even as they envy those outsiders who eventually make it into the inner circle. One woman, now in her third marriage, was discussing her will with her brother. The woman wanted to name her brother as the sole recipient of the assets of her estate. The brother was surprised and asked, "What about Tom (the third husband)?" His sister's reply, "He's a keeper, but he's not Family."

Frequently spouses are blamed for many of the problems in the family business. In many ways the spouse provides a mirror on the relationship between parents and children. Spouses can strip away parental intimidation, challenge habitual patterns of behavior, and look with disdain at the parents'/siblings' frailties and shortcomings. The result can create a dilemma for the child: challenge the traditional relationships and risk creating conflict, or assume the status quo and risk internal conflict with the spouse.

Family conflict is like a sore that, if realized and dealt with, heals and goes away. If not treated, family conflict can grow through inattention, lack of communication, poor judgment, and equivocation. An infected sore requires medicine, bandages, and attention. Sometimes surgery is required.

One of our clients owned a successful chain of retirement homes. Two married sons were active in the family business. One of the sons wanted to expand and acquire a local florist. The son argued that since his wife's family had been in the floral business, it would be a natural adjunct to their retirement homes. His wife was experienced and could manage the floral shop.

Dad agreed to finance the acquisition, and because he had always maintained equality between his two boys, insisted that the second brother and his wife also be involved. Ultimately, the two boys each owned a 50 percent interest in the florist. Each of the wives became active in the flower shop and jealousy between the two developed. The situation deteriorated and the two women ceased speaking to each other and communicated only through written notes. The situation spilled over into each family and began to affect the sons' relationship with each other. Dad was worried. He didn't know what to do. He depended on his sons' management of the business to provide for his retirement. He began to fear that his retirement—and the family business—were being threatened.

Actually, Dad created the problem when he insisted that the second son and his wife become equal partners in the floral business. Dad's solution was to discuss the situation with both sons and their wives who agreed to "undo" the ownership of the florist.

Son No. 1 bought out Son No. 2. Son No. 2's spouse was given a job in the retirement home. Within weeks, the two spouses regained their friendship. The boys' relationship, and the health of the business, improved noticeably.

RECOGNIZING PROBLEMS BEFORE THEY OCCUR

The box below lists a number of questions you should explore and discuss with various family members. Don't make the mistake of believing that because your situation is different, these are not, in fact, issues.

COMMON SOURCES OF CONFLICT

Succession

    WHO will be in charge?

    WHEN will it happen?

    HOW will it occur?

Participation

    WHO can/cannot join the business?

    WHEN can they no longer come in?

    HOW do you determine authority?

    WHAT preparation is required?

    WHAT if it doesn't work out?

Compensation

    WHO can own stock?

    HOW do you evaluate and pay family members?

Responsibility

    WHAT if there is a divorce?

    WHAT responsibility do you have to the community?

    WHAT responsibility do you have to long-term employees?

    WHAT responsibility do you have to other family members?

Source: John Ward, *Keeping the Family Business Healthy*

Children and their spouses may be reluctant to discuss certain business issues for fear of appearing self-serving or greedy to their parents. Mom or Dad should initiate discussion on these issues at a family meeting. While Mom or Dad are still active in the business, establishing rules about the issues raised in the list can help to prevent future problems when Mom or Dad are no longer around to referee. Changes to the rules require successors to act together, rather than against one another.

The physical setting for business discussions is important. Business problems discussed at home may be perceived differently from business problems discussed at work. Bringing up family conflicts during an evening discussion or around a dinner table is not conducive to an objective discussion. Set aside a time when all involved family members can attend a meeting to review business issues and concerns. You may not want to include spouses in the meeting unless they are also active or are shareholders in the business. However, while only those who are active in the family business should make the business decisions, it is important to follow up later with all family members to inform them of any decisions made.

A helpful exercise is to make a list of possible conflicts. By anticipating conflicts you may be able to head them off before they occur (see Form 4-1).

HAVING A FAMILY MEETING

It's possible that you've never had a formal family meeting to discuss business issues. A family meeting is similar to a corporate board meeting. An agenda is prepared in advance: a meeting date and time are established, and someone is appointed as recorder for the meeting. The "minutes" or notes of the family meeting create a record of the discussion and help establish continuity and communication among all family members, including those who cannot be physically present or active in the business.

It may be helpful to have an "outsider" present to keep the meeting from becoming one-sided and to ensure that all interested parties are represented. Intimidation in family relationships can spill over into family meetings. Trusted family advisors who attend may inadvertently favor one side against the other.

GROUND RULES FOR FAMILY MEETINGS

The list on p. 25 outlines four rules that should be in place prior to a family meeting. For an excellent book on conflict resolution, refer to Fisher and Ury's book *Getting to Yes*.[6]

One of the most difficult rules for people to accept is No. 4, "Personal compromise for the sake of the business." Choices may have to be made between decisions that benefit the individual versus decisions that benefit the business (postponing benefits to the individual). The "golden goose" (the business) should be protected if long-term results are everyone's goal. This assumes that the various attendees at the meeting are being honest regarding their intentions and objectives. If a family member refuses to compromise his or her position, other members may find themselves in the difficult situation of: (1). ignoring it and knowing that things will get worse, or (2). having to do something about it.

—————— **Form 4-1** ——————

What Possible Conflicts Could Occur
in Your Current Transfer Plans?

1. _____

_____

_____

2. _____

_____

_____

3. _____

_____

_____

4. _____

_____

_____

5. _____

_____

_____

6. _____

_____

_____

RESOLVING CONFLICT:
GROUND RULES FOR FAMILY MEETINGS

1. Attendees are PROBLEM SOLVERS:

   When we brainstorm solutions, we work together, not against one another.

2. Focus on THE PROBLEM, not the people:

   Accept the validity of the other's position.

3. Work to a WIN – WIN solution:

   Anything less (win – lose) is not acceptable.

4. Satisfy the UNDERLYING INTERESTS:

   Personal compromise for the sake of the business may be required.

Additional Tip: Having a mediator conduct the initial family meetings helps to keep the meeting focused on its agenda (purpose) and to defuse negative emotion (conflict).

When a family member's demands are ignored, the successful transfer of the family business to another family member may be jeopardized.

Caveat emptor: Resolution of the conflict may result in family members terminating relationships with the family or the business or having their business interests repurchased.

I hope you read this chapter prior to transferring any business interests to family members. If you have already transferred stock to family members, companion stock purchase agreements should be in place, in order to allow you to repurchase the stock.

THE "SQUEEZE OUT"

If you have transferred stock in your company to family members or even to key employees, you should be aware that minority shareholders have significant rights that can affect how you run your business and the business decisions you make.

In one recent situation, Mom and Dad gave away 93 percent of the value of the company to their five children while retaining the voting control for themselves. Although Mom and Dad controlled the company through their control of the voting shares, those shares represented only 7 percent of the value of the company. The total value of the company was about $15,000,000.

The children collectively decided that Dad, now 68, should retire and sought to squeeze him out. Dad could either: (A). take control of the company and oust the inactive children from the Board, thereby splitting the family permanently, or (B). negotiate with the children and seek a buy-out at an acceptable price. The children were willing to pay Dad only 7 percent of the value of the company, but Dad demanded considerably more to "get out." The emotional trauma that accompanied the negotiations made the transaction difficult and left irreparable scars within the family. By using offset funding methods described in Part II, we eventually bridged the "gap" between the two sides.

SYMPTOMS OF DISTRESS

Business and family systems send out signals if they experience distress. In the business, symptoms of distress are exhibited by customer dissatisfaction, low employee morale, high employee turnover, or a disproportionate amount of the owner's time spent in putting out fires and resolving conflicts, as in the above example. In the family, distress can be exhibited in drug and alcohol abuse, emotional flare-ups, poor communication, sickness, or apathy.

One of your first tasks is to evaluate the attention and energy both your business and your family currently receive from you. This will prepare you to determine the health of each system and predict potential areas of conflict. For example, one business owner wouldn't let go of his business because he would then be spending more time in an unhappy marriage with his spouse. More time at home was the last thing he wanted. Sometimes marital and family counseling are helpful in resolving "reentry" problems in existing relationships.

Wear and tear are expressed in various forms of aging, from plant and equipment repair to a decline in productivity. In the family, aging occurs as family members cease to communicate and become entirely independent of the family.

Although each system goes through a life cycle of birth, maturation, and "death," each in its own way "reproduces"—successors for the business, marriages and grandchildren for the family—and the system continues, although the configuration may change.

CHANGE IN THE SYSTEM

Business and family systems re-create themselves in response to challenges from the environment. The ability of your business to evolve new structures and functions may cause conflict for the business owner who feels threatened by change and doesn't recognize this need as a positive, evolutionary development. By simple definition, progress cannot occur when the status quo is maintained.

Business and family systems change as they self-perpetuate. The business system's ability to survive depends to a large extent on its ability to adapt to changing circumstances. The same applies to the family. Both will generate internal signals that, if listened to, offer guidelines for growth and evolution. Ignore the messages and both the business and family begin to decay.

In this stage of advance planning, the business owner should listen carefully and try to interpret the messages and signals sent by both the business and the family. Keep in mind that reception of these messages will filter through your own beliefs and attitudes. Your challenge is to be honest with yourself and to hear the messages objectively.

The recent growth of prepaid funeral plans exemplifies this objective listening. Although, historically, funeral directors have not marketed their services, consumers asked funeral directors to allow them to plan, and pay in advance, for their funerals. Recognizing the demand from the environment, some funeral directors not only listened, but have begun to actively promote this concept. These funeral directors can guarantee their businesses for the future through their preplanned and prefunded funerals.

In some cities, market share between competing funeral homes has shifted as a result of the preplanning arrangements. The funeral director who failed to listen and adapt will see a decline in business, while those who adjusted their policies and responded to the challenge from the environment will gain market share. The business's ability to be flexible and adaptable created dynamic new functions.

"Business" and "family" are more complicated. As times change, there is an increase in interdependence and complexity. Business and family life will never be as simple as "in the good old days." Computers and telecommunications now give us an instantaneous world view. Our boundaries are expanding.

For the business or family to survive, they must be organized to maintain an expanding world view. There must be greater commitment to efficient methods of communication. The already demanding responsibilities on managers and department heads will become even more complex. The current business owner may have succeeded by knowing his products, customers, and community. The next generation will need to understand not only these areas, but a much larger sphere of influence as well. As Ervin Laszlo writes, "To be 'with it' one must adapt, and that means moving along. There is freedom in choosing one's paths of progress, yet this freedom is bounded by the limits of compatibility with the dynamic structure of the whole."[7]

There are two messages here. First, the business organization of the future will require a leadership with a far-reaching view. This view can come from an outside Board of Directors, or from a less formal Board of Advisors. To map out the future of the family business, information and insight will need to be contributed by all those interested in its future.

Secondly, family members will need to develop professional competence to gain the respect of their peers, their employees, their customers and suppliers.

Family members should be able to rise as far in the business as they desire. Conflicts occur when the founder/owner puts a family member in a position for which he/she is neither prepared nor interested.

A 65-year old client has two children, a son and daughter. The son was active in only a small division of the family business. The daughter was not active and was married to a local farmer. The client was ready to transfer the business, but the son didn't want the increased responsibilities. He didn't want the business to be sold either. The daughter couldn't run it and agreed with the son that she didn't want the family business sold. They hired a general manager with day-to-day responsibilities for the overall company. The solution allowed Dad to let go, Son to keep his current position which he enjoyed, and Son and Daughter to maintain their shareholder roles without conflict.

In this example, success resulted from the *successors* deciding between themselves how to divide their parents' estate. The decision was made in a family meeting with all members present and participating. Here, the family system evolved the solution that allowed the integrity of the company to be maintained. The parents were flexible enough to allow the next generation to develop a solution that fit their needs.

SUMMARY

The successful transfer of a family business requires advance planning. For the transfer to succeed, the owner needs to evaluate the health of both the business and the family systems, as well as address potential areas of conflict that could arise.

Conflict resolution is achieved when both sides feel that they have "won." Try to remember that what's being negotiated are the business and its employees, and the quality of your product or service.

Creativity, flexibility, and immense patience are required. Stubbornness and inflexibility only raise the emotional ante in an already high-stakes game. Both the family and the business are at risk.

Conflicts are resolved through communication and negotiation, not by throwing dollars at them. The intent to resolve the conflict is as important as providing the solution that is ultimately implemented.

As we go forward, keep the following points in mind:

- The business, the family, and the environment are interrelated systems.
- Change is a constant element in these systems.
- Businesses go through cycles.
- Family members change and evolve.
- The environment (employees, customers, suppliers, advisors, the business climate) changes.

- Succession planning attempts to: (1). balance demands from these areas, (2). prepare the participants for change, and (3). reduce potential or actual conflict in the systems.
- Failures in succession planning stem from ignoring or not fully understanding differences in rules between the systems.

5

Recognizing the
Stages of Life

IN DEVELOPING A TRANSFER PLAN, THE BUSINESS OWNER SHOULD UNDER-
stand that as people pass through different stages in life, their business decisions
and values change, their relationships change, and their risk tolerances change.
Examining a potential successor to the family business is like examining one
photo out of a sequence of thousands, or like viewing a frozen frame in a video
tape.

A lack of perspective can result in a number of conflicts. Understanding general human behavior can provide security to the business owner unsure of his
younger successors.

Often it is very difficult for the 60-year-old business owner to remember
how he felt when he was 35. He may believe that today's young people seem
even younger than when he was their age, or he may feel that other 60-year-olds
seem much older than himself.

Similarly, it is difficult for the 35-year-old to understand many of the decisions made (or postponed) by the 60-year-old, particularly when those decisions
have an impact on the family-owned business. Age differences can have a significant impact on the successful operation and ownership transfer of family-owned
businesses.

This chapter will explore how values change as people pass through stages
of their lives, what those stages are, and how changing value systems affect business decisions.

An individual passes through five major adult life cycles, the first beginning at ages 25 to 30, and the last at age 60.[1] In each of these five life cycles, an individual acts and feels differently. Business decisions reflect particular life cycle stages. This can be particularly significant when a transfer of ownership occurs from one generation to the next. When different values and natural differences between the generations are not recognized, the transfer can lead to unnecessary conflict and potential failure. (See Table 5-1.)

EARLY ADULTHOOD

The first life-cycle stage, beginning at age 25 and lasting to age 40, is characterized as "early adulthood." During this phase, one goes through an initiation period in which the burdens of childhood are cast aside and the "child" becomes adult in his own way. This period can be characterized as novice adulthood, and possibly novice parenthood as well. It is a period of changing relationships with parents as well as with a spouse.

During this phase, institutional ideas are challenged and solutions are linked to personal experiences. Early adulthood is a time of personal gratification, which supports an emerging value system. It is during this period that the individual has the greatest energy, capability, and potential, and challenges the directions of the older generation. It is also a time of contradictions—past Pollyannaish illusions begin to fall away. Frequently these are replaced by a new cynicism directed at the traditions and practices of one's elders.

This type of behavior was exemplified recently at a meeting I had with clients and their 24-year-old son. The 24-year-old was very demanding in his relationship with his father. The son wanted immediate ownership of the company, not a gradual transference over five years. The son "needed more income" and "didn't want to work long hours."

As we discussed the situation, the son began to realize that he had limited business credentials and negligible financial strength. Why should his parents transfer the business to him? What skills does he bring to the table? What proposals does he have? What offers does he make? Why would a 60-year-old sell to a 24-year-old with no net worth?

Gradually, the father-son relationship began to change. The son, instead of demanding and expecting, began to see his position. And the father, instead of seeing the son as a demanding child, realized that he had to evaluate his son in a different light. The father recognized that the son was a key employee. As such, the father needed to spend some time preparing that key employee to handle the responsibilities of the business.

This 24-year-old typified most "early adults" who inherit or acquire a business. They want to grow and expand the business quickly. They seek capital for

_____Table 5-1. Lifestyles_____

		Effect On:	
Lifecycle	_Age_	_Personal Life_	_Business Decisions_
Early adulthood	30–40	• Initiation (Burdens of childhood)	• Interest in growing, expanding the business
		• Need for personal gratification	• Increase capital for expansion
		• "Novice" adult, husband, father	• Level or reduce retained earnings
		• Changing relationships with parents	• Higher risk tolerance
		• Full energy, capability and potential	• High debt tolerance
		• Contradictions and illustrations	• Low interest in personal retirement planning
Confusion (Mid-life transition)	40–45	• May seek mentor relationship	• May make significant business decisions
		• Time for major life choices (if not already made)	
		• The "invisible" son?	
		• Ultimatum vs. the "laid back" heir	
Middle adulthood	45–55	• Mental and physical changes: "aging"	• Build on foundations established in early adulthood
Confusion (Late adult transition)	55–60	• Compare accomplishments to dreams	• Keeping all options open
		• Confusion of purpose	• Propensity to do nothing
Late adulthood	60–70	• Must reduce heavy responsibilities of middle adulthood	• Increased interest in retirement planning
		• Moving out of center stage can be traumatic	• Less interest in expanding business
		• Part of the "grandparent" generation	• More interest in retained earnings
		• Give up authority or become tyrannical ruler	• Greater cash flow
		• Possibility of creative, wise elder with youthful vitality	• Lower risk tolerance
			• Lower debt tolerance

expansion and will "sacrifice" current earnings for future growth. They have a higher risk tolerance as well as a higher debt tolerance.

Early adults use business assets to leverage the business's growth, either through acquisition or through forward integration such as expanding into new markets or territories. Personal retirement planning often is of little interest because the cash needed to fund a retirement program might jeopardize future expansion opportunities.

MID-LIFE TRANSITION

The first mid-life transition occurs between the ages of 40 and 45 when major life choices are made. If the 65- or 70-year-old has not turned over the reins of the business, the 40-year-old feels stalled in development.

For counsel and guidance, the 40-year-old may seek a mentor relationship with a nonfamily member. The "child" who, until now, has taken a backseat in the parent's business decisions, begins to exert his influence. The parent's challenge, and opportunity, is to recognize the offspring's contributions and give him the leeway to implement his own ideas. Alternatively, the parent can neutralize the son's or daughter's contributions by undermining their efforts, thus risking the offspring either leaving the business or seizing control by force.

If a "child" leaves the business between the ages 40 to 45, generally there will be hard feelings on both sides. Nothing positive is accomplished. The owner has lost his potential heir at a time when the owner needs to know and feel secure that the heir is in place—however unprepared he may be. The son loses a business opportunity, but may choose freedom and independence over vacillation and insecurity on the part of the current owner/manager.

One client chose the neutralization route when he rendered his son "invisible" by telling him that he had the power and authority to make and implement decisions and then undermined him behind his back. This occurred during a three-year transition period. Since Dad was still active in the business, the older key, nonfamily employees would come to Dad every time the son made a decision or a request with which they didn't agree. Dad, reluctant to confront his key employees, would tell them to continue doing things as they always had and to ignore the son. When the son would confront Dad on these issues, Dad would apologize and promise to stop negating the son's efforts. Nevertheless, the pattern continued and the son eventually became a nonentity in the firm. The son's growing sense of worthlessness created tremendous internal conflicts. Although he wanted to continue the family business into the third generation, he wasn't sure how long he (and his wife) could withstand the emotional turmoil. Increasingly, freedom and independence became more attractive alternatives to this particular business opportunity.

MIDDLE ADULTHOOD

During middle adulthood, between ages 45 and 55, the individual builds on the foundations established during early adulthood. With business expansion programs now in place, his attention can focus on creating a strong management team and an organizational structure.

Day-to-day operational responsibilities for the business should be delegated to the key management group. Sensitivity to key employees' needs is important, and additional compensation and recognition programs should be explored. During this period, credit lines become well established and banking relationships mature and are solidified.

On the personal side, mental and physical changes associated with "aging" become more noticeable. Physical stamina, endurance, and attention spans begin to lessen. With an increased likelihood of stress- or age-related illnesses, internal messages become all-important. During middle adulthood, family members should understand what, if any, opportunities exist within the business; leadership and lines of authority should be discussed and established.

LATE-ADULT TRANSITION

Near the end of middle adulthood, the individual enters a period of confusion, the late-adult transition. Between the ages of 55 and 60, the phrase "I'm burned out" can be heard repeatedly. Accomplishments are compared (not always favorably) to dreams, and a confusion of purpose exists.

One day the business owner wants to build new branches; the next day, he wants to sell the business to the first prospective buyer. During this period of confusion, the business owner wants to keep all options open. This is admirable on the surface, but unfortunately, the result is usually a propensity to do nothing. This static state can delay indefinitely a transition to the next generation.

During this period, financial and strategic planning are particularly critical. Yet this is the time when the owner is most likely to procrastinate making any decision, thus running the risk of entering the next phase with no business plans, no successors, no management team, and eventually, no more options.

One client described the effect of aging on business decisions this way: "You become somewhat apprehensive at the age of 60. You wonder about your health, whether you are still doing a good job, and whether your children agree with what you are doing. You have all these questions and very few answers.

"You begin to lose confidence in yourself. You lose confidence in other people, and you begin to feel more insecure. I feel far less secure this year than I did when I was 50 or even when I was 55 or 57. And I worry that by the time I'm 65, I'm going to feel very insecure and I won't really know what's happening any more. Then by the time I'm 70, I may be so insecure that I won't be capable of making any arrangements with my children."

Clearly, middle adulthood is a period of strategic thinking and decision-making. Unresolved issues create fragmentation and inconsistency that can prevent present and future business owners from reaching their highest potential.

LATE ADULTHOOD

Beginning at age 60 and continuing to about age 70, the fifth cycle, late adulthood, occurs. During this time, the business owner is interested in personal retirement planning. He has less interest in expanding the business and sees growth programs from the "not with *my* dollars" perspective. The owner's interest in building retained earnings is now of tremendous importance, since the owner looks at the business financial statement as a personal savings account. During this period, there is greater cash flow in the business since cash is being accumulated instead of being put to work. There is less risk tolerance and less debt tolerance. The business owner looks forward to paying off the mortgages (if he hasn't already) and not encumbering business assets further.

During late adulthood, the heavy responsibilities incurred during middle adulthood should be reduced. Nevertheless, for the unprepared 60-year-old, suddenly leaving center stage can be a traumatic experience. Now is the time that transfer strategies should be complete, or the owner risks the possibility of becoming a tyrannical ruler, stalling his successors, and threatening the long-term growth and success of the business.

Business owners who are in their early to mid-70s are often so comfortable that it's too late for them to let go. They prefer the status quo. They don't like to change and they don't like anything that threatens their concept of security.

If you are in your early 70s and you haven't already made plans to transfer the business during your lifetime, if there is change, it is going to be initiated by the younger generation. You may resent the younger generation's ideas, although you "know" their reasons and "understand" their rationale. Emotionally, it is easier to preserve things as they are and let the estate planning take its course.

The situation of a 68-year-old client of ours is illustrative. He has a 40-year-old son and two other offspring. When the son asked us to talk to his dad about the importance of transferring the ownership, the son was concerned that he would become partners with his inactive brother and sister. Because the business represented the bulk of his estate, Dad had been reluctant to plan any transfer strategies for fear of being unfair to the two inactive children.

As we resolved equalization for the inactive children, we were able to address the more important issue: the necessity of transferring the business before Dad became recalcitrant. Although Dad insisted on having the transfer accomplished over a three-year-period, while he was still 68, Dad entered into purchase options with his son. The son (or the corporation) had an automatic "call" to purchase the stock from Dad.

The transition went smoothly for the first two years. But recently the son called to tell us Dad regrets letting go of the business and is beginning to change his mind. The son has done nothing wrong ("It's just that Dad doesn't like change anymore"). The son, however, is protected by the purchase options and is therefore able to proceed with the transition and the continuity of the business.

SUMMARY

When you started your business, you assumed risk, you had energy, and you persevered in the face of adversity. Now, in spite of overwhelming odds, you've succeeded and your business has survived and grown.

As you confront passing the torch, your challenges are different. They are more personal in nature. The environment to be "conquered" is internal rather than external. The challenge is mental, not physical or economic. It involves teaching rather than doing, sharing and communicating rather than making unilateral decisions.

If the independent business is to survive and grow into the next generation, extraordinary efforts will be required by all those involved. The wisdom acquired during late adulthood and the energy of early adulthood must work together to ensure a smooth and successful transition.

The 60-year-old who understands life cycles can capitalize on these changes to teach (and share the accomplishments of) the next generation.

6

Establishing the
Family Commitment

In order to successfully transfer your business, an extraordinary commitment to your successors is required *by you*. Is this a surprise?

Most owners believe the commitment is required *from* others. Our clients say, "I'm already committed to the business and have been for the past 32 years! It's the successors I worry about." However, your commitment is *to* your successors, not the business. Without a personal commitment on your part, the transfer of the business will be jeopardized—and may never occur.

One client asked us to intervene between his son and a son-in-law. The son-in-law had asked for a 50 percent interest in the business in order to stay with the company (after Dad retired). The son responded, "If you give Son-In-Law a 50 percent interest, I'm leaving!"

Dad was sure the dilemma couldn't be resolved and, I believe, secretly hoped the son-in-law would leave. Dad was surprised to learn we were successful in having son and son-in-law reach a compromise regarding their future ownership. On learning of the reconciliation between son and son-in-law, Dad was distraught and agitated rather than relieved. He even talked of firing the son-in-law. Although Dad *said* he was committed to retention of the designated successors, his behavior indicated otherwise. A reconciliation of all parties, and open lines of communication, allowed the business to remain intact.

COMMITMENT FROM FAMILY MEMBERS

Personal commitment *from* family members *for* the business is critical for the system to maintain itself in a healthy state. Family members' commitment to the business helps the family system by binding it to a common purpose. Without this commitment from the family, transfer of the business to a family member has a significantly greater chance of failure. When family commitment is unavailable, the business owner should consider bringing in professional managers, or sell the business to employees or a third party.

Commitment is more than mere obligation. It requires fire-in-the-belly energy. In the midst of planning with one client, a hidden fear that we commonly hear emerged, ''They don't seem to have the drive; there isn't any intensity,'' he lamented.

Some business owners have noted that the children come to work at 8 and want to leave at 5; the current owner may believe the business requires an on-the-spot 24-hour commitment, 7 days a week. Perhaps this kind of thinking needs some revisions. If the next generation is more efficient, with professional managers that can help accomplish some of the responsibilities, perhaps the seven-day week is unnecessary.

Our experience has shown that the actual time commitment on the part of the next generation is really not the parent's concern. Rather, their concern is for mental and emotional commitment to the business. For parents to feel comfortable with the next generation's ownership (or with the employees who are buying out the owner), the new owners may need to exhibit a shift in their priorities. Business requirements take precedence over other matters, but that doesn't necessarily require the owner's on-site presence 7 days a week, 24 hours a day.

The sophistication and competitiveness of most businesses today require an awareness that extends beyond an 8- or 9-hour period. The commitment that causes concern at the current owner level is that, too frequently, the children turn their brains off when they leave the business each day and don't turn them on until they come in the front door again the next morning.

When the brain is left in the ''on'' position at all times, it is easier to take advantage of opportunities that may arise on weekends, during social occasions, when reading the newspaper, or while on vacation. Such opportunities cannot be capitalized on when the mind is turned to ''off.''

One of our clients does his best thinking while vacationing in Florida; another has his best brainstorms while on the golf course. The creative process cannot be forced. It occurs spontaneously and unexpectedly. The commitment sought by the current generation is for the next generation's brain to remain in ''on'' whether at work, home, or on vacation.

Another level of commitment is that of the spouse. In one family meeting, I met with the son and his wife, a successful marketing associate for a large computer company. While we were discussing conflicts between the son and son-in-law, both of whom were active in the business, the spouse commented, ''I don't even know why I'm here. I work for a large company and I leave my problems at

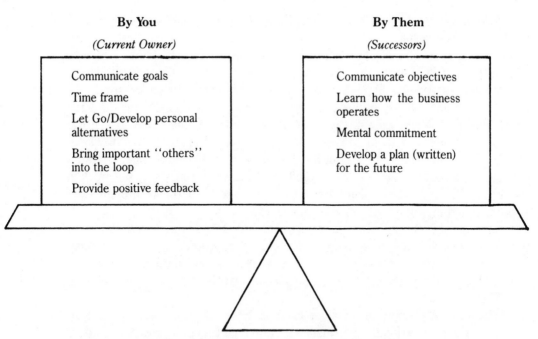

By You	**By Them**
(Current Owner)	*(Successors)*
Communicate goals	Communicate objectives
Time frame	Learn how the business operates
Let Go/Develop personal alternatives	Mental commitment
Bring important ''others'' into the loop	Develop a plan (written) for the future
Provide positive feedback	

Fig. 6-1. Commitment required by current owner and successors.

the office when I come home.'' What's missing here? One spouse fails to understand the pervasiveness of a family business. Both spouses must be aware of, and carefully avoid, the potential push-pull this situation can create. (See Fig. 6-1.)

PREPARING A BUSINESS PLAN

Do you have a business plan? Very few family businesses have a written business plan. Usually Dad acquired the business (or started it) and has successfully operated it for so long, in the same fashion, that writing a formal business plan seems unnecessary.

Periodically, a business opportunity comes along that gets Dad's attention. The opportunity may be consumer-driven, the result of a technological change, or initiated by a family member, associate, friend, or employee. After some analysis, Dad decides whether or not to capitalize on the opportunity. For the purpose of our discussion here, it is important to note that Dad did not seek the opportunity—it found him.

Without a long-term game plan, it is difficult to determine the proper response to a new idea, new product, or new investment. Lack of a business plan can seriously hamper transferring the family business.

Without written business goals, it is hard to have a sense of personal accomplishment, since results achieved can match goals that were never set. Consequently, there's a tendency to "hang on" to the business and strive to achieve still more, long after those responsibilities should have been shifted to others.

A business plan should be prepared in conjunction with the successors; otherwise, it is impossible to evaluate the successor's goals and ideas for the business. Too often when we ask the successor how he or she plans to run the business, we hear, "The same way Dad has done it." While this may work for Dad, it is not always as successful for the successor. Times change. Markets change. Customers change. What worked for the past 20 years may not work in the future. The business plan forces the successors to think through—and express in writing—how they plan to run the business.

Although you may be eager to transfer the business to the next generation, be careful. Require the presentation of a plan. It can protect you and your business. If you and your successors are unsure what to include in the business plan, the American Management Association has an excellent workbook and self-study instructional.[1]

While the successors are developing their business plan, you, the current owner, should be developing the Business Transfer Plan. In it, you should identify certain "trigger" dates, including:

- Dates when you want to begin transferring ownership to others
- Dates when you would like to have this completed
- Dates when "control" is shifted, i.e., over 51% of ownership of voting interests
- Dates when 100% (or the balance) is transferred
- Dates when responsibility for day-to-day operations shifts
- Dates when you no longer intend to be "full-time"

This timeline will help you determine the amount of time you have available to train your successors.

SUMMARY

Studies indicate that fewer than 5 percent of all start-up family businesses ever actually appoint a next-generation owner/manager. Herein may lie one explanation for the small business perpetuation rate.

How can family businesses be successfully transferred when the next-generation owner/manager is never even appointed? Are decisions regarding the ownership of the business revealed in documents that become effective only after the owner's death? How can the next generation continue to give the kind of commitment required when they are unsure of their status within the company.

Make a commitment to your successors. Give them every opportunity to succeed. That will be the only way you will learn if they can handle the challenges they will surely face.

It is better for you to find out *now* if your successors are ready to accept the business responsibilities. Otherwise, your widow may learn the successors are incapable after you are no longer around.

7

How to Let Go

AS CAROLE DESCRIBED THE PROBLEM, THEY HAD ESTABLISHED FINANCIAL priorities such as security and wealth, but they had never established priorities for personal happiness. She and her husband had started with nothing and worked 40 years to reach their present situation—in a rut because they can't let go of the business. Personal assets are more than $1 million in cash and investments. In addition, Carole and Paul hold notes for another $600,000, their ownership in the business is worth $1.7 million, the profit sharing plan has $400,000 in Paul's account, and there are miscellaneous other personal assets. Carole and Paul live in a 6,000-square-foot house on 3 acres, including a lake and a boat dock. They haven't used the boat this year. They only used it once last year.

Paul was asked what a transition meant to him. He answered, "We lack direction. We have no management in the business, no overall game plan, no strategy." Paul wants to transfer the business to his son, but is concerned that the son "won't do it my way."

The transfer of the business is neither a financial nor a tax issue. The most difficult aspect in the business transfer occurs when the owner must confront the transfer of power and decision-making to the next generation. Inherent in this transfer of control are fears that the next generation will do things differently—perhaps better—and when the current owner "lets go," he may be forgotten and purposeless.

This chapter will explore some of the emotional bridges to be crossed in business transfers. Many financial advisors spend a great deal of time structuring the financial aspects of business continuity: tax planning the transfer, creating retirement and pension plans in favor of the current owner/manager, and ensuring that he or she is financially secure. The underlying issue of how the transition will actually be accomplished on a day-to-day basis is never addressed, and the practical problem of business continuity is ignored. Existing owners may be preoccupied with the transfer of the ownership, while their children are more concerned with the day-to-day operations—the control and the management that ensure a healthy and profitable business.

The issue of letting go may be even harder when the sale is to a third party. I was recently involved in a transaction where the owner of the business sold to a conglomerate for more money than he ever thought his business was worth. At the seller's request, the transaction included continued active involvement of the present owner. He was 56 years old, not ready to retire, and thought he could make a meaningful contribution to this large publicly held company by running his now newly acquired branch. He was eager to be an employee of the firm.

Within 90 days, this particular client called to say they were the worst 90 days of his life. The parent corporation didn't respond to his memos and didn't run the business as he had. The corporation didn't follow the procedures he felt they should follow, and they didn't get involved in the community as he had. My client's problem was that he never mentally let go of the business.

When a business is sold or transferred to family members, to employees, or to a third party, in all likelihood, the new owner is going to run it differently. If the new owners are interested in the current owner's ideas, they'll ask, and they may or may not listen to the answers. Letting go is crucial to the future success of the business and to the mental health of the owners, both past and present.

LETTING GO THE EASY WAY

There is an easy way to let go: by transferring ownership in stages, over time so that, ultimately, the next generation will own up to 49 percent of the business. Potentially adverse income tax or estate tax consequences are addressed in Part II. The purpose of discussing a partial transfer here is to address it from an emotional and psychological aspect.

When considering a transfer over a two- to three-year period, you will need to examine your motives and determine if you are making a real commitment. If the ultimate ownership to be transferred is 49 percent, then there is no real commitment or risk as long as you retain that 51 percent. With 51 percent ownership, you are still in control. You can watch your successor and if he makes a mistake, sell the business out from under him; there was no contractual commitment to transfer the whole business to him. As long as you neglect to train your successor, you fail to accomplish the transfer. Granted, if your successor owns 49 percent, you have transferred part of the value of the business to someone else. However, in a sale to a third party, the owners can recover part of that 49 percent through creatively structuring compensation arrangements or noncompete agreements.

The 49 percent path is the easy way out; after three or four years, if the successor doesn't meet your expectations, you can sell the controlling interest to someone else. The risk is not assumed by you, the owner, but rather by the person to whom you have partially transferred the business.

Consider Tom, the 42-year-old son of one of our clients. Tom had worked in his father's business for 20 years. If Dad gives Tom 49 percent of the business over the next three years, Tom will then be 45 years old, too old to be hired by another business. Dad could still sell his controlling interest to someone else or hang on to the controlling interest until he dies. Clearly, Tom is at risk.

Tom got married a year ago. His wife is 32 and they now have a baby. Tom is concerned about his future. "If Dad had made a real commitment," he says, "then I would know that I am the true heir. I could make my own decisions and enjoy the satisfaction and rewards from being an up-and-comer in the community." Alternatively, without Dad's commitment, Tom is just another employee and minority shareholder. He has no assurance that actual control of the business will ever be his. Promises, yes. Contractual agreements, no.

LETTING GO—THE ROAD LESS TRAVELED

The alternative to partial transfer represents a more emotional risk. More than that is a communication risk: opening up and sharing, teaching, and educating. Total transfer means turning over the reins of the business, committing now to the future by working with the successor, allowing him to make mistakes, guiding him patiently, and training him to become a successor in more than name only.

The 100 percent business transfer, contractually legalized, can also be spread over a three- to five-year period. In this case, the commitment is both emotional and contractual. One business owner wanted desperately to transfer the business to his son over a three- to five-year period. This plan became a rewarding experience as he watched and helped both his son and the business grow. To achieve this kind of peace, the owner recognized and accepted his new role as consultant and advisor, rather than doer. Now he was the teacher instead of the boss, and he let his son, the "student," make his own decisions—and mistakes. The emotional risks were as great as the emotional rewards for both the father and the son.

Another business transfer solution is to sell the entire business outright, and with it, the management problems and day-to-day decision-making. Most business owners can come up with creative reasons for selling the business to a third party. A common thread running through this rationale is that the owners believe the heirs are not ready to receive control of the business.

One of our clients convinced himself that because his son had gotten divorced three years earlier, the son wasn't ready to assume control of the business. Because the parents are disappointed that the son's marriage failed, they are withholding stock from him.

Interestingly, the son confided that during the 15 years of his marriage, he was depressed and lacked ambition. He lived in his father's shadow and his father never felt threatened. Now that the son is successful in his second marriage and no longer living in the shadow of his father, he is more career-oriented and has his own ideas about his father's business. Dad doesn't like this "new" son as well. Transferring the business now makes Dad feel vulnerable.

Nobody likes to have their decisions, business or personal, challenged. A number of business owners are unwilling to risk the emotional turmoil they are sure will result from 100 percent transfer of the business.

CONTROL

The issue of control and identity are important in business ownership. Only one person is ultimately responsible and accountable for day-to-day operations. Frequently, it is these day-to-day decisions from which the owner/manager derives a sense of self-worth and ultimately, a sense of security and well-being.

Often business owners haven't developed lifestyle alternatives outside the business. Some have unhappy marriages and prefer to spend all their time at work. Others truly don't know what to do for relaxation. Work is their security blanket.

The hardest part of transferring the business is relinquishing control. As the spouse of one client noted, "My husband will think twice before he gives up his control of the business. He's always called the shots." The wife compared her husband's control of the business to her role as homemaker. "If I had a full-time housekeeper and had to adjust to the housekeeper's needs for running the home, I would feel as though I had lost what had been mine. I derive my identity from my responsibilities for the home."

Control and identity do not have to be inseparable. One solution lies in achieving a sense of self-worth from more than one source, including family and hobbies as well as the business.

DO YOU KNOW HOW TO HAVE FUN?

If positive alternatives to work haven't been discovered by the time you are 60 or 62 years old, it becomes difficult to leave the business.

LETTING GO

- Does it Mean Bowing Out?

- Dying in the Saddle Isn't Good for the Horse.

- What does a Chairman of the Board Do?

- Begin to create Positive Alternatives.

- Our Cultural Values Should Include Gaining Wisdom.

One client's dilemma is illustrative: "Nobody is going to drill a hole in your head and pour in fun. I'd like to retire, but I'll admit I haven't developed an alternative to long hours at the office. I'm not sure that my wife and I know how to have fun. I wish we had explored other interests when we were younger."

The potential "black hole" of age 65 can be a beginning rather than an end.

Your next-generation owner/manager should become president of the firm with responsibility for management of day-to-day activities. You, the retiring owner/manager, now promoted to chairman of the board, should no longer work directly with any of the employees to avoid undermining your new president's authority and responsibility. As chairman of the board, you become responsible for establishing long-range plans for growth of the business. Implementation of those plans is carried out by the president. While you and the president confer daily, implementation of activities is always the president's job.

You receive weekly reports from the president and work with him to increase revenues and to research demographic and market changes. Your time is now free to become the best spokesperson the firm can have. Maintaining contacts with possible acquisition candidates in the community represents one method for future business growth, as well as potential sites for expansion. In addition, you can prepare and motivate the president for implementation and management of any expansion programs.

One of our clients successfully accomplished his chairman-of-the-board status by moving his office out of the firm. Employees could no longer go to him for day-to-day decisions. The new office is a block away from the business. In the new office is a "war board" on which is outlined seven or eight long-term business strategies and tactics for achieving those plans. Business responsibility is allocated to each of three sons who are active in the business. The three sons report to the chairman regularly. The four of them meet to discuss day-to-day progress and to decide how to achieve the long-term business objectives.

Successful business transfers begin with the owner's assessment of the present situation and decisions on what will be in the best interests of the business. This success necessitates relinquishing authority and moving from center stage, allowing the offspring to assume the business's major responsibilities.

SUMMARY

Without resolution of personal issues associated with risk, control, and self-worth, even the best business transfer plans will not succeed. Take a few minutes to answer the following questions to determine your own situation.

- Are all participants ready, willing, and able to commit the time and energy that is necessary for the business to remain successful?
- Are all the participants willing to compromise in order to reach a workable solution?
- Has a realistic time frame been established with "benchmarks" or mileposts along the way?
- Will a change in control mean a change in ownership?
- Have plans been communicated to all family members (active and inactive)?
- Have plans been communicated to all key nonfamily personnel?
- Has the current owner learned how to enjoy leisure time?

The following briefly summarizes the appropriate roles of the chairman of the board. He:

Does Not	Does
Fish all the time.	Establish policy and see that the president implements policy.
Wash windows.	Ensure quality maintenance.
Sit on the front porch and rock.	Work in the community as a PR person for the company.
Keep the grandchildren.	Make sure that communication among family members is maintained.
Become a couch potato.	Do long-term strategic planning for the company.

8

How Much Do You Need to Retire?

"ALL I NEED IS BAIT AND GAS MONEY FOR THE BOAT," SAID A MICHIGAN BUS-iness owner.

In this chapter, we will discuss personal financial planning. Your financial dependence on the business must be recognized and resolved before you can afford to withdraw.

While most family business owners take enough money out of their businesses to lead a comfortable lifestyle, they often fail to create any other significant assets in their estate. Family business owners with significant assets are frequently beneficiaries of inheritances. A few have been successful in passive real estate or other investment opportunities. Seldom does the business owner consciously diversify his net worth by creating outside assets.

There is some rationale to this short-sighted approach. The successful and profitable business may represent the best investment the owner has. He knows the company and its markets, the officers and the employees, and feels comfortable that the business's direction will assure future success. Rarely does the owner have time for the same amount of due diligence with other investment opportunities. The owner considers his increased earnings and profits in the business as "my best investment."

A potential problem occurs when the owner begins to consider passing the business to successors and realizes that his "money" is locked inside the business.

Two important questions need to be addressed: How much of the business value is needed for personal support after the ownership is transferred? Second, does the business provide financial opportunities to children who are not active in the family business? Should it?

DISTINGUISHING FINANCIAL DEPENDENCE FROM BUSINESS VALUE DESIRED

During their working years, Anne and John have sufficient income to either meet or exceed their standard of living. But they can't afford for the income stream to stop. During retirement, their income needs continue with inflation, yet unless the business is sold, their source of income may have dwindled.

Determine your financial "dependence" on the business by calculating the amount of money you will need from the business after you transfer ownership. You should maintain your present standard of living for the remainder of your life and your spouse's life.

IMPACT OF INFLATION

Figure 8-1 graphically illustrates that the consumer price index equalled 100 in 1967. By 1988 the consumer price index was equal to 354.6. For every one dollar of goods and services in 1967, the same goods and services cost $3.55 in 1988.

If inflation was zero, the $50,000 you live on today would allow you to maintain the same standard of living. However, at the present rate of inflation, that is unlikely to happen. Figure 8-2 shows us what 5 percent inflation will do to our $50,000 in 20 years. Let's say you are 55 today. With 5 percent inflation, in 20 years you will need $132,000 to buy the same goods and services that you buy today for $50,000. And when you are 85, you'll need an income of $216,000 to maintain your $50,000 standard of living. (See Fig. 8-2.)

WHY FINANCIAL PLANNING IS SO IMPORTANT

Personal financial planning is critical as it relates to the transfer of the business and your long-term financial security. Income during retirement may be affected by several factors, including longer life expectancies, changes in tax laws, and inflation. Additionally, every financial plan should consider the following implications:

1. The ever-increasing complexity of investment and savings vehicles require more time, effort, and technical expertise than most people can or will devote to managing their own funds. The result can be a loss of earning power on investments, which, in turn, may be important in funding future income requirements.

2. Retirement and fringe benefit packages provided by the company are complex and affected by changing tax laws. Retirement packages are often not implemented as part of an overall transfer strategy that provide the greatest financial benefit for the owner.
3. We are living longer. To provide inflation-proof income during retirement may mean staying with the business longer than is appropriate.
4. New insurance products continue to proliferate and, although important to financial planning, are often not properly understood.
5. Changes in our tax laws, deems the consideration of tax-sheltered, tax-deferred, or tax-free vehicles important.

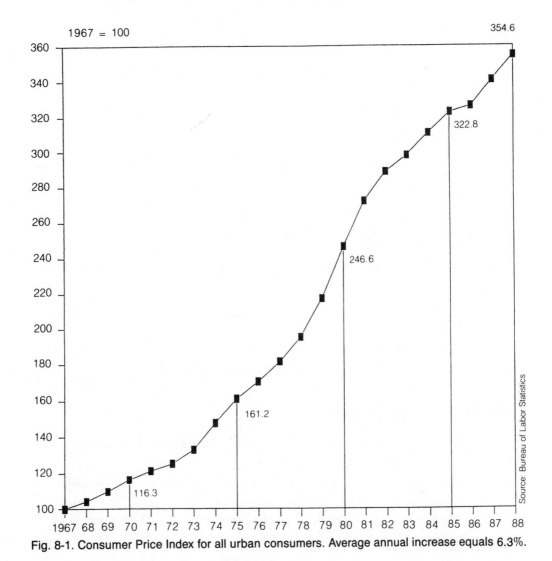

Fig. 8-1. Consumer Price Index for all urban consumers. Average annual increase equals 6.3%.

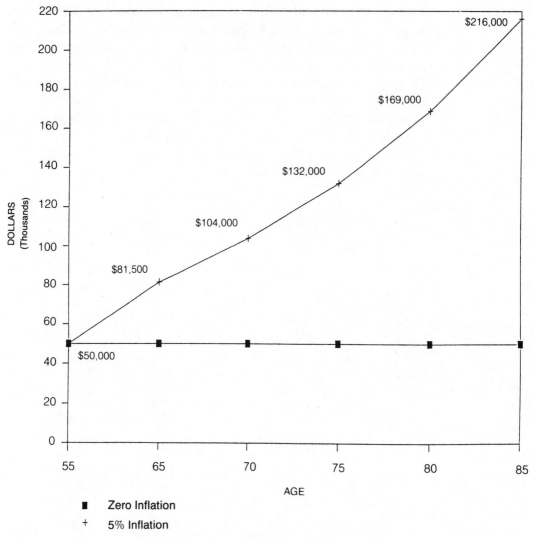

Fig. 8-2. The effect of inflation on purchasing power.

WHY SO MANY FAIL TO PLAN

People neglect to coordinate personal planning with the transfer of the business for a number of reasons, predominately:

- *Procrastination*—As people devote more time and money to short-term needs, they defer consideration of long-term financial planning. The failure to act can be the biggest hurdle in reaching financial goals. There is never a "right" time to start.

- *Indifference*—Failure to seriously consider both long-term needs and develop a personal financial plan. Some people just enjoy the lack of planning and discipline. For them, the time, energy, and discipline required to develop and maintain a financial plan is too big a burden.
- *Neglect*—No one really cares to look at the possibilities of death, disability, and retirement. By ignoring these possibilities, maybe they will go away.
- *Invincibility*—No one will always be employed nor live forever.
- *Ignorance*—Failure to understand and apply the tax laws, failure to understand the concept of purchasing power, failure to understand how money can and must compound to meet financial needs.

HOW MUCH DO I NEED TO RETIRE?

The explanations, tables, and worksheets in Appendix A should help you calculate your own financial requirements, what you will need to retire, and how financially dependent you are on the business.

There are five questions you will need to answer before you can determine your need:

1. **At what age do you expect to retire?** Although retirement may not mean full withdrawal from the business, it may mean a change in your income as you currently know it. In any event, it will be necessary to determine how much you will have in investable assets at your retirement age.
2. **What interest rate do you want to assume?** The assets at retirement age will be consumed or paid out over the life expectancies of you and your spouse. Therefore, you should choose a conservative interest rate to avoid outliving the income stream. If you intend to live only on the interest from your investments, it will be necessary to have a larger amount available in order to provide an income stream that protects your principal. On the other hand, if you deplete the principal as well as the interest, there may not be anything left for children who are not active in the business. Chapter 19 explores equalization strategies between those who are active, and those who are not active in the business, and how such strategies can affect your estate planning.
3. **How long do you and your spouse expect to live?** No one enjoys predicting their mortality, but you can get some idea of your life expectancy by averaging the mortality of your parents and your spouse's parents. Be conservative and protect yourself against outliving your resources.
4. **How much do you need each year to live comfortably?** If the business is paying for a lot of your personal expenses on a deductible basis, it

may be difficult for you to calculate exactly how much money you will need to live on. Your ability to provide for your financial independence is predicated on your having sufficient income and assets to prevent outliving your resources.

Lifestyle changes must also be considered. If you've been unaccustomed to traveling or taking long vacations and would like to do so during retirement, you'll need to identify an amount for annual travel expenses. If you plan to buy a condo (or sell one), that must be taken into account. Gifts to grandchildren should be planned, as well as extraordinary purchases of art, antiques, cars, jewelry, and so on.

Although most people don't become spendthrifts after they retire, many have an opportunity to enjoy some of the things they postponed while they built their business. Others maintain the same lifestyle they always enjoyed.

5. **What rate of inflation do you expect over the remainder of your life?** The higher the rate of inflation that you choose, the more conservative will be your projection, since it will require you to have more funds at retirement age. Refer again to Fig. 8-1 and the increase in the consumer price index from 1967.

CASE STUDY

John and Anne are each 55 years old. They currently need $75,000 per year *in today's dollars* to support their standard of living. If they both retire in 10 years when they turn 65, they will need an inflation-adjusted $75,000 for as long as they both live. In addition, after John dies, Anne will need $50,000 (in today's dollars) for as long as she lives.

In planning for their future, Anne and John must consider the after-tax rate of return, before and after retirement; inflation; and life expectancy.

As illustrated in the chart on p. 57, Anne and John's needs continue to increase, even as their income sources decline. Anne and John's sources of income were provided through compensation from the business from ages 55 to 65; after that, Anne and John depend on retirement benefits or income from personal assets throughout their projected life expectancies of age 90. The difference between the "sources" line and the "needs" line represents Anne and John's financial "dependence" on the business—i.e., the amount, either in a lump sum at age 65 or in a stream of payments, beginning at age 65, that John and Anne need to maintain their current standard of living. If there is any surplus saved after Anne and John satisfy their annual living requirements, the money will be available to their heirs. If there is a shortage, Anne and John will run out of money. Anne and John have 10 years, beginning at age 55, to begin accumulating some of the funds they will need during retirement.

HOW MUCH DO I NEED TO RETIRE?

Data

John age 55.   Anne age 55.

They need $75,000 per year in today's dollars. If both retire at age 65, they need an inflation-adjusted $75,000 for as long as they both live.

She needs $50,000 per year if he dies, for as long as she lives.

Factors

1. After-tax rate of return
   Before retirement/After retirement

2. Inflation

3. Life expectancy

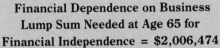

**Financial Dependence on Business
Lump Sum Needed at Age 65 for
Financial Independence = $2,006,474**

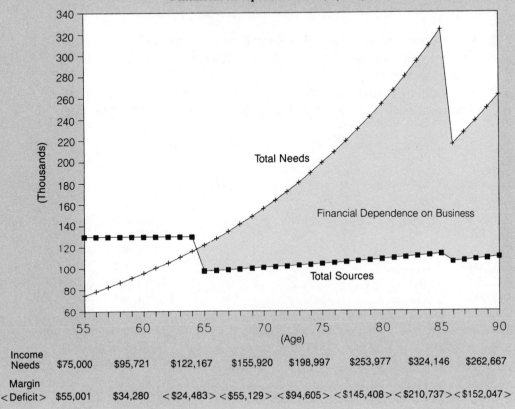

Income Needs	$75,000	$95,721	$122,167	$155,920	$198,997	$253,977	$324,146	$262,667
Margin <Deficit>	$55,001	$34,280	<$24,483>	<$55,129>	<$94,605>	<$145,408>	<$210,737>	<$152,047>

Anne and John have two choices if they want to keep the business in the "family": begin now to accumulate funds in the business and have some of the "dependence" funded when they reach age 65; or at age 65, fund their "dependence" by selling the business to children or key employees, and rely on future payments to support retirement.

Instead of being dependent on a future income stream, John and Anne could elect to sell their business for cash to the children or their key employees. The lump-sum amount of cash needed to fund the deficit through their 90th year is $2 million, net after taxes.

It is unlikely that Anne and John's business will be able to afford a cash buy-out. Without the buy-out, however, the transfer may be jeopardized. John and Anne may be forced to sell the business to an outside third party. But, if John and Anne can be made financially secure (as we'll explore in Part II) and assured of receiving their payments, an installment transaction from the successors is acceptable and keeps the family business in the family.

OPTIONS TO RETIREMENT NEED

John and Anne have other options. As shown in Table 8-1, there are several variables that affect the amount of money they will need at retirement:

1. **Their standard of living.** If John and Anne decide to live a reduced standard of living, the amount of money they will need at 65 will, of course, be affected.
2. **The rate of return on investment.** Both preretirement and post-retirement can have a significant impact on the amount of money needed.

Table 8-1. Options to Retirement Need

Today's Standard of Living	Age of Retirement	Inflation	Rate of Return	Life Expectancy	Present Value	Present Value at Age 65
$75,000	65	5%	5%	90	$1,726,757	$ 2,812,706
$75,000	65	8%	5%	90	$3,212,532	$ 5,232,583
$75,000	65	5%	8%	90	$929,386	$ 2,006,474
$75,000	70	5%	5%	90	$1,748,014	$ 2,847,330
$65,000	65	5%	5%	90	$1,496,523	$ 2,437,678
$65,000	70	5%	5%	90	$1,514,945	$ 2,467,686

You can control:
- *Rate of Return*
- *Age of Retirement*

You can't control:
- *Inflation*

You don't want to control:
- *Standard of Living*
- *Life Expectancy*

Varying the rate of return by as little as one percentage point can have significant results.

3. **Inflation.** If inflation is slightly higher or slightly lower than anticipated, it can also affect the amount of funds Anne and John have. Higher inflation requires more dollars to satisfy their standard of living. Conversely, low inflation assures that money will be left over and goods and services can be purchased at a lower price than expected.

   By structuring the transfer to include an inflation adjustment, Anne and John can protect themselves against some of these variables by building hedges into their strategy.

4. **Age of retirement.** John and Anne may elect to work longer; rather than retire at age 65, they may decide to retire when they are 68 or 70. Delayed retirement provides additional income from the business for another three to five years. Although the inflation-adjusted dollars Anne and John will need at retirement may be slightly higher, there will be fewer years required for those payments to be made.

5. **Life expectancy.** If, instead of assuming life expectancy to age 90, Anne and John assumed age 85, or age 95, the amount of dollars needed would be affected.

SUMMARY

Understand and anticipate your personal financial requirements. Whether you are independent *of* the business or dependent *on* the business for your financial well-being can have a significant impact on your decisions and your timing in passing the torch.

Calculating your needs and providing methods to cover your financial requirements allows you to make business decisions without the burden of being financially dependent on the next generation of owner/managers.

9

Keeping Your
Key Employees

THERE ARE A NUMBER OF REASONS WHY EMPLOYEES PREFER TO WORK IN A family-owned company rather than a large bureaucratic organization. Family-owned businesses tend to be more flexible and provide greater access to the owners. In the family-owned business, people are treated as individuals, rather than bottom-line numbers. Caring is communicated one-on-one, not through a human resources department. In many cases, the family-owned business is less rigid about the number of hours spent on the job or the few extra days of vacation.

Relationships with key employees and the attitudes they have about the business's successors can have a significant impact on the success or failure of a transition effort. The following is from an actual situation. Do you recognize any similarities to your own business?

The Williams Company is a classic owner-son transfer. Roger, the son, is 30 years old, bright, married, motivated, energetic, committed to caring for his parents, and comfortable with estate equalization, handled for Roger's sister with other assets. Don Williams, the 62-year-old father, wants to gift his stock to his son over the next five years. Doug, a cousin, owns 5 percent of the stock, and the keyman, Joe, owns 16 percent of the stock.

Don gave Joe 100 shares of stock 20 years ago. Joe is 46 years old and has worked for the business for more than 30 years. One day after a planning meeting, Joe, Doug, Roger, and Don discussed Don's plans to gift his stock to Roger over the next five years. Joe said, "I've been working with Don for 30 years; I was working here before Roger was born, and the thought of Roger as my boss makes me feel as if I've been demoted.''

Joe left the room, and Doug explained Joe's reaction, "A few years ago a friend pointed out that even though I run a branch operation in another town, I have the freedom to make my own decisions, set my own budget and pay the bills as though I own the company. But the friend cautioned me not to be fooled into thinking that someday I would own this business. Roger is involved in the business and someday his father will turn it over to him. That's when I realized that someday I would work for Roger. I can accept that because I get along with Roger, and Roger doesn't interfere with my branch office.

"When I told Joe about my friend's observations, Joe didn't listen. Now as Joe hears the reality of Roger's succession, Joe feels threatened. It's too bad Joe doesn't realize that if we help Roger succeed, it can only increase the value of our own stock.''

Exactly what should a keyman expect, particularly one who has been involved and active in the same business for 30 years?

Many of Joe's coworkers think that Joe creates his own problems. He tries to control the weekly staff meetings and is negative, domineering, and sometimes obnoxious. Yet Joe's coworkers recognize that he has given 30 years of his life to the business. Were Joe's expectations of someday owning the business realistic? Probably not, particularly since Roger has worked there for 10 years.

What is realistic for Joe? Ten years ago, when he was 36 years old, he could have left the business. Now he is 46 and it will be more difficult for him to find another job with comparable compensation.

Joe's problem is one of perception, coupled with unrealistic expectations. Doug, the cousin, is a family member, yet he understands that he will never own the business. Because Doug's perception about the business and the family relationships is clear, he has realistic expectations that cushion him against disappointments.

Do you have unrealistic expectations about family members? Do your key people, your "adopted" family members, have unrealistic expectations about their future role with the company? Are your children realistic? Have any of you ever discussed any of these transition issues?

Communication plays a crucial role in your employees' and your family expectations about the future. Promises, innuendos, and off-hand remarks made under duress or frustration can lead to faulty perceptions and inaccurate expectations.

In the situation with Joe, his challenge will be to overcome his perceptions. Joe has the opportunity to work with an energetic, bright 30-year-old (Roger), who has good ideas but needs some guidance. Perhaps most importantly, Roger also needs Joe's wisdom, the wisdom of someone with 30 years of experience in the business. And Roger needs Joe's support. Together, the two of them can build the business and in so doing, increase its value and the value of its stock. By the time Joe turns 60, his stock could increase ten-fold. If Joe sits back, waiting and hoping that Roger will fail, Joe's "action" will be self-defeating. Roger's failure becomes Joe's failure and the situation becomes one of financial lose – lose.

In addition to clarifying expectations, communication is important in painting a vision of what the business can achieve with the key employee's support. In describing your business plan to your key employees, you can help those employees understand what their role will be in the company's future. This can help you compete with large organizations that may offer better employee compensation and benefits. The need for communication with key employees, and for creatively motivating them, is particularly important during the business's transition from one generation to the next.

Communication and motivation extend from day-to-day appreciation of employees to creative financial incentives that encourage employees to remain with the family firm. If the next generation has valid reasons for not keeping all of Dad's key people, early retirement or other programs may become an option.

In this chapter we will address incentives designed to retain key people when the business is being transferred *within* the family or between families. If the business owner is considering selling or transferring to key employees, the issues are different and are explored in Chapter 20.

One of the easiest and simplest ways to express appreciation for an employee is to say, "thank you." Recently, I talked with employees in a family-owned service business. Their most common complaint was a perceived lack of personal appreciation. In all other cases, employees ranked the owner high on compensation paid, benefits provided, and flexibility of work hours. The one thing missing was the pat on the back.

Like Don, some business owners have chosen to give stock ownership to key employees as a way to "tie them in" and reward them for their service and performance. However, nonfamily stock ownership may backfire as you begin your succession and estate planning and consider the possibility of bringing your children into the business. Having a nonfamily minority shareholder can create compensation, business valuation, and retirement difficulties. On the other hand, a buy-out may prove to be an expensive cash proposition at a time when the money is needed to buy out the owner or expand the business.

NONQUALIFIED PLANS

As an alternative to using stock, other financial incentives can stimulate key employees to remain with the company. The programs differ depending on what and for whom you are trying to provide and reward. These plans are called *nonqualified plans*.

It is important to note the distinction between nonqualified plans and qualified plans. *Qualified employee benefit plans*, including pension and profit sharing, require that the plans be designed in accordance with various tax laws (ERISA in 1974, and later amendments in TEFRA in 1982, DEFRA and REA in 1984, and the Tax Reform Act of 1986). It is customary and advisable to seek advance approval of qualified plans from the IRS.

Nonqualified plans allow the employer to provide benefits to key employees who have either exceeded the limits for qualified plans or wish to augment their already existing company benefits. These additional benefits can be provided by the employer on a discretionary basis to one key individual, or to many. The benefits can be designed as retirement plans, death benefit plans, phantom stock, or stock option plans.

Nonqualified plans are further distinguished from qualified plans in that they do not need to be currently funded by the employer. Because unfunded plans are exempt from all ERISA requirements, the employer need not seek advance approval by the IRS. However, if the plan is funded, ERISA's reporting and disclosure requirements and fiduciary rules must be met and the funded plan is subject to ERISA enforcement provisions.

Benefits received by participants from unfunded, nonqualified deferred compensation arrangements are exempt from taxation until received. Similarly, the employer is not entitled to a tax deduction until the employee is taxed on the benefits.

A comparison of the different features between qualified plans and nonqualified salary continuation and deferred compensation arrangements is shown in Table 9-1. The nonqualified plan is often referred to as a "discriminatory benefit plan."

SERPs AND DEFERRAL PLANS

The most popular type of nonqualified plan is a Supplemental Executive Retirement Plan (SERP). The SERP is especially attractive for older, key employees who may feel insecure or threatened by the next generation's/successor's unproven skills. It is during this transition period that the support of key employees is most needed.

Providing a SERP to selected key people can send several messages:

1. The company is sensitive to employees' personal retirement needs.
2. The company wants to relieve employees of any financial insecurity they may anticipate with the proposed changes.
3. The company wants to encourage key people to remain with the firm until normal retirement age.

_____Table 9-1. Qualified vs. Nonqualified Plans_____

	Qualified Pension or Profit Sharing	Nonqualified Salary Cont. (SERP)	Nonqualified Deferred Compensation
Does the employer receive a current tax deduction?	yes	no	no
Can the plan discriminate in favor of highly compensated employees?	no	yes	yes
Is the Internal Revenue Service approval required?	yes	no	no
Who establishes the ground rules?	the gov't.	you	you
Will the deposits be available to the company in the event of an emergency?	no	yes	yes
Will the benefits be forfeited by the participant if he/she terminates employment?	ltd.	yes	no
Are there likely to be annual administrative costs and fees?	yes	ltd.	ltd.
Will Internal Revenue Service and Department of Labor filing and reporting forms be required?	yes	no	no
Can the plan be terminated for any reason whatsoever without Internal Revenue Service approval or tax penalty?	no	yes	yes
Can the corporation recover its costs of funding benefits?	no	yes	no
Is a bond required?	yes	no	no
Is there fiduciary investment responsibility?	yes	no	no

One of the indirect, but very real, benefits of a SERP is the additional financial security provided for older employees, allowing them to retire at the standard retirement age. Often, successors want to respect the current owner's relationships with key employees but don't want the financial burden of carrying employees who may be an unnecessary expense to the company. The SERP provides the financial security many employees need during retirement.

There are generally two types of SERPs: "Excess Benefit" and "Top Hat." Excess Benefit plans restore benefits to key people who may have lost some benefits through curtailments in qualified plans. For example, assume you want to recruit a 50-year-old senior executive for your company. If this executive terminates his existing employment, he may lose significant benefits available under his current retirement plans. For that reason, he may be unwilling to change jobs. What can you do? The Excess Benefit SERP can provide that individual a full replacement of all retirement benefits he lost when he terminated his current position.

A Top Hat plan provides salary continuation to enhance post-retirement income for key people. A Top Hat may provide a fixed annual benefit or a percentage of the employee's annual or final pay. There are no limits on the benefits you can provide.

With the properly designed SERP, the benefits are received as a supplemental pension by the employee and do not jeopardize or reduce social security or other benefits the employee may be eligible to receive.

A SERP can be provided *on a discriminatory basis* to key employees. The benefits can be different for each participant. Benefits in the Top Hat SERP can "wrap around" and be received in addition to any qualified pension, profit sharing, or 401(k) plan benefits. Top Hat SERPs do not jeopardize any other benefits that are currently offered. The participants in a SERP plan can be in a special class that is different from the rank and file.

SERPs may be "informally" funded or can be an unfunded liability of the employer. Since the participant in SERP benefits becomes a general creditor of the company, the SERP is usually informally funded. Any contributions to an informally funded SERP remain an asset of the employer. If the employee terminates employment prior to reaching normal retirement age, the employee could forfeit all benefits in the SERP at the election of the employer. Vesting is at the discretion of the employer.

Deposits to the well-designed SERP grow tax deferred until payout. Then the employer receives an income tax deduction as benefits are paid to the participant, and the employee recognizes income at the same time. During the years of participation in the SERP, the employee does not recognize any current income nor pay any income tax.

Finally, one of the most important features of the informally funded SERP is Cost Recovery. *After* all benefits are paid to the participant, the employer can recover the entire corporate cost of funding the program from the SERP account—either after the benefits have been paid or at the time of the employee's death.

Here's an example of how an informally funded SERP can work:

John Smith is a 40-year-old manager making $35,000 per year. ABC Company is contributing $3,500 per year to his profit sharing account but wants to do more for John. By depositing an additional $3,000 per year to a SERP account for John's benefit, ABC can provide John, at age 65, approximately $25,000 *per year* for 10 years (based on current interest and mortality tables), *in addition* to any profit sharing benefits John receives. At the end of the 10 years (John's age 75), ABC will recover the $75,000 they invested over the 25 years they funded for John, while John receives $250,000. Adjustments can be made to recover the entire cost plus interest. And if John leaves ABC before age 65, he forfeits the entire SERP benefits.

SERPs are easy to install and administer since there are no IRS and very few Department of Labor filings required by ERISA. While social security and qualified retirement plans (pension or profit sharing) may provide retirement income for all employees, a SERP can enhance post-retirement income for a special group of key employees with a very low cost to the employer (due to cost recovery).

SERPs are different from Deferral Plans (see Fig. 9-1). Deferred compensation plans allow employees to defer the receipt of earnings to later years. Some accrual is often added to the deferrals based on an interest rate or company performance. These plans appeal to employees who do not need additional, current taxable income and are willing to defer the income—and the taxation—to a later time.

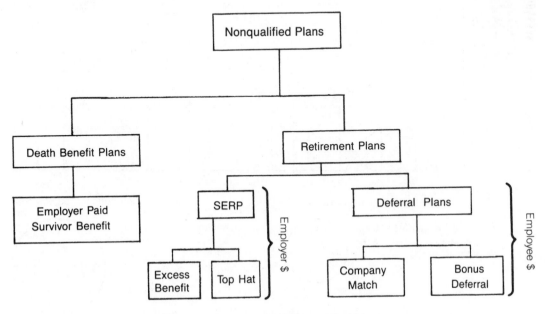

Fig. 9-1. An overview of nonqualified plans.

One caveat is that in order for the employee to avoid the constructive receipt of income and not be taxed currently, the employee becomes an unsecured, general creditor of the employer. The compensation deferred must be subject to a risk of forfeiture on the part of the employee; if it is not, it will become immediately taxable. Through the use of a grantor trust, this risk can generally be eliminated and taxation still avoided until benefits are received.

Deferred compensation plans provide a tax benefit through deferral; in order to turn this into a financial incentive to remain with the company, the company can provide a "matching" feature. Benefits provided by the company under the matching portion can be forfeited if the employee terminates before normal retirement age. With the company match, the difference between the nonqualified plan and the 401(k) is that the nonqualified plan can be discriminatory, while the 401(k) cannot. (See Fig. 9-2.)

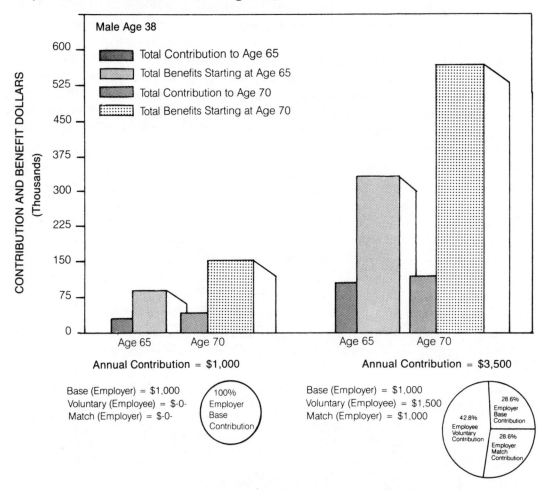

Fig. 9-2. "Golden Handcuff" with and without matching feature. Manager's incentive plan, including contribution and benefits.

SHARING GROWTH WITH KEY EMPLOYEES

SERPs and Deferral Plans are extremely effective for retaining and motivating older employees. Both provide a benefit that acts to supplement qualified retirement plans. In some cases, however, younger key employees would prefer compensation arrangements indexed to the growth or performance of the company. Sometimes the key employee is tempted by equity-related plans in public companies. The dilemma the business owner faces is in matching the offer without giving up stock in the closely held business. Phantom stock plans and stock options are two methods of sharing growth.

Phantom Stock Plans. "Phantom" stock is exactly what the word implies. Although no stock is transferred, the employee is entitled to the appreciation of the stock as if he actually owned it. The participant is granted appreciation rights to a number of shares. The appreciation in a share may be defined by book value or some other indicator of company growth. As Fig. 9-3 shows, the executive receives a cash payout of the appreciation in the shares at the end of a specified period. The payout may be tied to normal retirement age and be paid as a supplemental retirement benefit. Whereas the SERP provides an identifiable, fixed benefit (a fixed annual amount or a percentage of pay), phantom stock plan benefits are contingent on future performance or growth.

Timing	Years	
	1	5
Phantom Stock	Grant ━━━━━━━━━━━━━━━▶	Payout
Book Value:	$20	$50
Employee Investment:	$ 0 ━━━━━━━━━━━━━━━▶	$ 0
Employee Tax:*	$ 0 ━━━━━ ($30 × 0.28) ━━━━━▶	$8.40 (Tax Due)
Employee Gain (After Tax):	$ 0 ━━━━━━━━━━━━━━━▶	$21.60 (Net Gain)

*Assumes the employee is subject to a maximum tax of 28 percent.

Fig. 9-3. How a Phantom Stock Plan works.

Many private companies with phantom stock plans use the change in book value of the common stock as an index of company growth. Other companies seek an annual independent valuation of the stock to calculate the changes in value of the phantom shares on a per-share or per-unit basis. An independent valuation may determine the fair market value of the shares more accurately and may be a better measure of how well the employees achieved their objective of increasing the value of the company.

Stock Options. Stock options are not as common in family businesses as in other organizations, since the grant of the option gives the nonfamily employee the ability to buy stock in the family company. Current ownership can be potentially diluted.

Nevertheless, two types of stock options exist: *nonqualified* and *incentive* stock options. The differences between these two plans are summarized in Table 9-2.

Table 9-2. Incentive VS. Nonqualified Stock Options

	Incentive Stock Option	Nonqualified Stock Option
Tax on purchase?	NO: Income is deferred until shares are sold.	YES: The amount subject to tax is the difference between the exercise price and FMV on date of exercise.
How is gain treated?	Capital gain by exec., no deduction to corp.	Ordinary income by exec., corp. gets deduction equal to income reported by exec.
What determines value of options when granted to exec?	Fair market value (for exec. to qualify for capital gain treatment).	Any price set by Board of Directors.

BEING CREATIVE

Real estate in a key employees' benefits package can be especially effective for mature businesses that do not expect rapid growth (which could be rewarded through phantom stock or stock option plans). Real estate is a unique way to attract talented managers, or to retain key people.

The real estate benefits concept is a bonus plan using a Tax Code section that allows compensation to be paid in real property instead of in cash. In return for services rendered, the key group receives equity in real estate as current compensation. The plan continues over a period of time until the key employees completely own the property. The value of the equity is determined by annual appraisal and is reported as income by the participants and deducted as compensation by the company. The company and its executives share any income, operating expenses, and depreciation deductions pro rata according to the percentages of ownership.

The executive is "vested" in the equity contributions as he receives them. If he terminates employment or retires, the company can repurchase the executive's interest in the property at the current market price. The repurchase can be paid out over a period of time to the executive. Life insurance may be used to fund the company's purchase in the event of the executive's death.

If the property is residential or located in a resort area, the executive can use it for 14 days or 10 percent of occupancy (whichever is greater) each year. One property can be owned and used by several executives or by a key group.

If vacation property is used, you may want to make it available to middle managers and other nonkey employees for their vacations. The company deducts the fair market rental value of this time as compensation to the nonkey employees, and the employees recognize the value of the week's rent as income. (See Fig. 9-4 on p. 72.) As an example, let's assume the value of the week's rent is $1,000. Assuming a 28 percent tax bracket, the employee's cost is only $280! Although the employee recognizes income of $1,000, his only out-of-pocket cost is the *tax* on the income, i.e., $280.

This same program can be applied to resort or office condos, raw land, or other investment opportunities, including business expansion or acquisition.

SUMMARY

To a large extent, a successful transition depends on the support of key employees. Since the key group has spent many more years of service in the business than the successor(s), some extra benefits or financial incentives may facilitate the employees' support of the next generation. As existing employees retire or terminate, it is also important for the next generation to have incentives that can help them recruit their own key people.

The addition of nonqualified plans to key employees' existing benefit programs can enable you to select and reward these individuals for their loyalty, commitment, or performance. Nonqualified plans are extremely flexible and can be individually tailored to each situation. The provision of "golden handcuffs" through forfeiture conditions can deter key individuals from leaving the family firm.

The retention of key personnel, and their support for the successors, can go a long way toward smoothing a bumpy transition and significantly enhancing the success of the next generation.

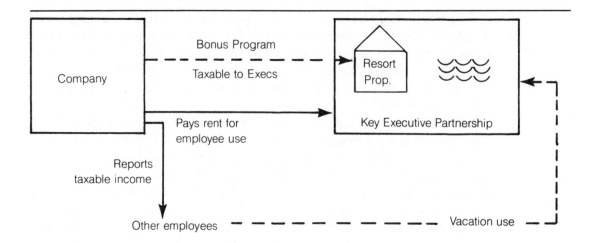

Benefits to Execs

Rent paid by corp for other employees' use creates positive cash flow.

Execs can have limited use.

Property appreciation belongs to Execs, pro-rata according to ownership.

Can list property in exchange networks and trade time for properties in other location.

Benefits to Corp

Bonus program to Execs creates tax savings with no cash out.

Company's share of depreciation expense creates tax savings.

Offers unusual benefit to key group as "golden handcuff."

Offers benefits to other employees who have vacation use of property at bargain rates.

Fig. 9-4. Using real estate.

No matter which program, or combination of programs, you provide your employees, it is also important to remember to communicate with them and to reiterate the advantages of working for a family firm.

When keeping key people during a period of transition, keep in mind the following:

- Be aware of their concerns for:
    - —Job safety
    - —Health of the business
    - —Personal financial security
- Are they "managers" or "workers"?
- What role can they play to smooth the bumps during a transition?
- How could they obstruct/sabotage your plans?

- Will the business survive without them?
- What if they leave to compete with you?
- Bring them ''into the loop'' regarding your plans for the business.
- Create financial incentives (''golden handcuffs'') so they can help *you* achieve *your* goals.

10

What You
Can Do Now

IN THIS CHAPTER, I'VE OUTLINED SEVEN PRIMARY ISSUES THAT OFTEN BECOME
major obstacles in transferring the family business. Before we can proceed to
Part II and discuss transfer strategies, it will be important for you to address
each of these issues, establish your position, and communicate it to others.
Overcoming these seven obstacles and taking positive steps will do more than
anything to help you transfer the business to the next generation successfully.

The following summarizes the seven issues and the action items that are
needed now.

Issue	Action Needed
1. Goal Setting	Set clear personal and business goals, establish time frames, and communicate those goals to important others.
2. Family conflict	Understand differences between business and family systems. Hold regular family meetings with those who are "active" in the business.
3. Life cycle	Learn to empathize with people who are at different stages in their personal and professional lives.

Issue	*Action Needed*
4. Commitment	Examine your personal commitment to others before you ask them to make a personal commitment to you.
5. Letting Go (of control)	Develop positive alternatives so trauma will be reduced.
6. Financial independence (or the lack of)	Diversify, and build up assets outside of the business.
7. Key employees	Recognize the ''nonfamily'' member's personal concerns over continuity and solve them before problems arise.

Part II

Transfer Strategies for Your Business

11

What's Your Business Worth?

WHAT IS THE VALUE OF THE BUSINESS TO YOU? LOOK AROUND AT THE tangible assets: the real estate, buildings, machinery and equipment, and rolling stock. You should also include the intangibles, the loyalty and dedication of employees, your manufacturing processes, the quality of services you provide, your customer base, your business reputation and standing in the community, patents on products, and new technologies. Although it is difficult to quantify these "intangibles," they are an important part of what makes up your business.

Before you transfer the business, it will be necessary to determine a particular dollar value that represents "your company." There are other questions you'll need to address. Is the company worth more than its assets? Is it worth more than its retained earnings? Are there future opportunities waiting to be realized by the new owners? Are the earnings or cash flow from the business predictable and steady? Do you anticipate these earnings will continue in the future?

Placing a value on your company in order to transfer it to children or employees may be a difficult task. Although you may know everything there is to know about your company, you may have no idea of its true worth.

The question of value becomes more complicated when you attempt to put a price tag on it. The price can vary depending on the circumstances: The selling price to your children may be less than the price you would ask from a large company that was attempting to buy you out. The determination of value can be motivated by other reasons as well. To reduce potential estate taxes, you would want your attorney to argue to the IRS that the company has minimal value. If there are currently stock purchase or buy/sell agreements, which establish a selling price for your shares, the agreements may not reflect the value you believe the business is worth.

Although value can be subjective, objective resources are available to help in determining worth. When you want to know the value of your car, you consult the Kelly Blue Book, for prices on all makes, models, years, and options of cars and trucks. The Blue Book can tell you what to expect from the sale of your car, or what to pay for the car you are considering purchasing.

The assets of your business can be appraised by an outside third party. A value will be established for your machinery, your real estate, your furniture and fixtures. An appraisal of the business assets, however, does not take into account the "intangibles" discussed earlier. How do you measure creativity, loyalty, or relationships? An appraisal of assets ignores "synergy," the whole that is worth more than the sum of its parts. The difference between the "wholeness" of the business and its individual components/assets also has to be valued to get a true representation of what the business is worth.

VALUATION METHODS

A business valuation is essentially an attempt to predict future events: the growth or contraction of the business, the rate of inflation, the appreciation of real estate and other asset values, and the anticipated costs and expenses of running the business. The predictions are based on historical and financial records of the business, your judgment as an owner, the expertise of the valuation firm, and other knowledgeable resources.

There are several methods commonly used in determining a value for the business:

- Book Value, as reflected in the company's financial statements.
- Adjusted Book Value reflecting adjustments made to book value to more accurately reflect the current value of the company's assets.
- Standard Valuation Methods used by national and regional acquisition companies for valuing target companies.
- Capitalization of earnings methods used by the IRS and the courts in valuing business interests for estate and gift tax purposes.

Book Value

Book value is the historical value of the assets of the business, less the company's liabilities, as recorded on the company's books and reflected in the financial statements.

_____ **Table 11-1. Smith Enterprises, Inc.; Business Ownership** _____

There are many ways to value a business. Any of these approaches might be used to value the stock, depending on the purpose of the evaluation.

| | | | _____ _Values at 12/31_ _____ | | | |
Stockholder	# of Shares	% of Shares	Buy/Sell Agreement at Book Value	Adjusted Book Value	Industry Standard: 1.5 times Gross Revs.	Capitalized Earnings Method
Bob Smith	3,500	87.5%	$771,750	$967,750	$3,937,500	$2,362,500
David Smith	350	8.8%	$77,175	$96,775	$393,750	$236,250
Brett Adams	150	3.8%	$33,075	$41,475	$168,750	$101,250
TOTALS	4,000	100.0%	$882,000	$1,106,000	$4,500,000	$2,700,000
Per Share Value			$220.50	$276.50	$1,125.00	$675.00

In the hypothetical example in Table 11-1, the book value of Smith Enterprises, Inc., was adjusted to eliminate any nonoperating business assets or liabilities. Nonoperating business assets would be investments, notes held, or assets that are unrelated to the primary activity of the business.

Adjusted Book Value

The adjusted book value is the book value, as described above, with accumulated depreciation on assets added back. Adjusted book value represents the original undepreciated cost of assets and is more meaningful in a company with newly acquired assets, or assets that hold their value, than in a company that has held assets for many years.

Industry Standard

The industry standard valuation in Table 11-1 is based on a formula used by acquisition companies in an industry in which Smith Enterprises operates. Real estate may or may not be included in the formula. In the Smith Enterprise example, the value was calculated as one and one-half times gross revenues, averaged over the past five years, which includes the fair market value of the real estate as determined by appraisal. By contacting the executive director for your own trade association, you may find "rules of thumb" that can be applied to your own business.

Capitalized Earnings Method

An important factor affecting business value is the earnings potential of the business. Will the business generate an attractive investment rate of return from the purchase of business assets? How will the "intangibles" such as goodwill impact your rate of return?

The capitalized earnings method is the method most accepted by the IRS for estate and gift tax purposes. The method attempts to quantify the goodwill of the company in terms of its earning power, over and above the value of operational assets. Our example in Table 11-1 determined a value based on five years' historical earnings. These were taken from the financial statements of Smith Enterprises, adjusted to eliminate nonoperating revenues or expenses. It also included adjusting the officers' compensation to a reasonable and customary salary consistent with salaries paid in the industry.

The capitalization of earnings approach requires you to determine an appropriate rate of return and then multiply or "capitalize" the average annual earnings of the company by that number in order to determine the company's earning power. Factors to be considered are the reputation and longevity of your business, your market share, cost of labor, and various risk factors. An example of risk to be considered would include the extent of the company's success based on personal relationships with the owner. If the owner died or was no longer involved in the business, the value of the company could be dramatically affected. If a management team is in place, it would enhance value by reducing risk. In other instances, risk of future competition or technological obsolescence must also be considered and factored into the expected capitalization rate.

By examining historical earnings, a "trend" can be discerned; that is, are the earnings growing, deteriorating, or remaining level? Have there been extraordinary events which have occurred, such as an acquisition or divestiture, sale of an asset, or money spent on R and D? "Quality" of earnings can be identified through such an approach and can be a useful predictor of the future of the business.

The valuation that is developed is based on financial statements and other information that you, the owner, provide. The estimation of value is according to formulas developed by the evaluation firm you use. Different results can always be obtained by someone using different opinions, methods, or formulas. According to the method the IRS would be more likely to use, a value of $675 a share, which is more than three times their buy/sell agreement price, is established. (Refer back to Table 11-1.)

STOCK PURCHASE AND BUY/SELL AGREEMENTS

When you acquired your business, started your company, or transferred shares to others, you may have entered into stock repurchase agreements (or buy/sell agreements) with other shareholders. Often these agreements do not reflect current values. They may be based on book value, or adjusted book value, calculations. If a formula approach is used in the agreement, it may adjust the per-share value of the stock on a regular basis. However, it may also be restrictive in the assumptions used in the underlying formulas.

Value based on stock purchase agreements are not automatically accepted by the IRS. You should be cautious, especially if the value is tied to "book" or "adjusted book" value.

A "red flag" may be raised when a transaction for book value is among family members. The IRS challenge questions whether the transfer represents a transaction for less than full consideration. The IRS might consider this a gift. The difference between fair market value and the value at which the business was transferred would be subject to gift tax. An understated value in an estate would reduce the IRS' share of tax from the estate. When nonfamily members, such as an unrelated key employee, are a party to the agreement, it supports the position that the agreement was entered into as an "arm's length transaction."

Even though the IRS may not agree with you, they don't always win if the case ends up in court, as the following true example illustrates.

The founder of Hallmark Cards died in 1982. The corporation was family-owned and its shares were never listed or traded on a public market. Mr. H's stock was subject to various transfer restrictions and buy/sell agreements that called for a sales price of "adjusted book value." The stock had never been purchased or transferred at more than this value and had been subject to the buy/sell agreement since 1963. Payment terms were 10 percent down, with the balance due over nine years at 5 percent interest. The estate hired two major brokerage firms to value the stock. Both said the stock was worth approximately adjusted book value. The IRS thought otherwise and hired its own expert business valuation firm. That firm was told to ignore the buy/sell agreement's effect on value, but it did apply a 5 percent discount to reflect the lack of marketability associated with the closely held company. The adjusted book value resulted in an estate value for the stock of $135 million, while the IRS expert found the value to be $307 million, or approximately $112 million in additional estate taxes.

The Tax Court couldn't ignore the buy/sell agreement and found that a purchaser of Mr. H's stock could not have forced Hallmark to go public, which would have been required to realize the IRS' $307 million value. Further, the Tax Court found that the estate's appraisers had done their job in comparing values of similar companies to Hallmark. The estate's value was upheld.

ESTABLISHING THE BUY/SELL AGREEMENT PRICE

In "Buy/Sell Agreements and Appraisals," Orville B. Lefko writes, "Almost by definition, the setting of a value for a business to be covered by a buy/sell agreement is an essential feature of that agreement. Too often it is also the most neglected feature of the agreement, set in an arbitrary, unprofessional manner—almost as an afterthought."[1]

Setting a value for a buy/sell agreement is difficult because no one knows when an event that triggers the agreement will occur. The agreement should cover death, as well as disability and voluntary or involuntary withdrawal from the business.

There are three basic approaches to developing value in a buy/sell agreement:

1. Negotiation among the parties.
2. Some type of formula based on the financial statements. This could be book value, adjusted book value, capitalization of earnings, or some combination of those variables.
3. Independent outside appraisal.

The formula approach is difficult to use because, once the formula is established, it is frequently not reviewed for accuracy in later years. Business conditions can change, capitalization rates can change. If the formula is not reviewed, years can pass until some event triggers a redemption. Then the dismayed shareholders find that the price established does not reflect the original intent of those who developed the agreement.

Another common problem in agreements is the lack of clear definition. Even when the agreements specify the purchase price at book value, it may be difficult to define book value. For example, is book value calculated as of the date of death, the end of the month preceding death, the last regular accounting period, or the end of the fiscal year of the entity?

HYPOTHETICAL CASE INVOLVING BOOK VALUE

Smith Enterprises, Inc., a service company, has three shareholders: Bob Smith, who started the company; David, his son; and Brett Adams, a key employee. Bob Smith owns 87.5 percent of the stock, and his son and key employee own the balance. There are 4,000 shares outstanding. The book value of the company is $882,000. This is a per share value of $220.50 each. The buy/sell agreement between Bob, David, and Brett, and Smith Enterprises is pegged at book value. This is the price that Bob, David, or Brett would receive in the event of death, disability, or withdrawal from the business.

The company has some depreciated equipment and machinery; when the depreciation is added back to book value, the "adjusted book value" of the company is $1,106,000. The per-share value becomes $276.50, a 25 percent increase over the book value price. If the assets of the company had remained equal to their original cost (without considering their appreciating in value), the book value price used between father, son, and key employee discounted their interests by 25 percent each!

Smith Enterprises is a member of a national trade organization. Bob, a former president of the trade group, has been approached by acquisition companies who realize that Bob will soon be retiring. Through his industry contacts, Bob finds that the same acquisition firms have approached his associates with similar-size businesses in other parts of the country. The "industry standard" value is based on a rule of thumb that is roughly equal to one and one-half times gross revenues, including the fair market value of the real estate.

Smith Enterprises currently grosses $3,000,000, which would mean a value for the operating company of $1,125 per share for each of the shareholders. This is more than five *times* the price identified in the buy/sell price agreement. In other words, unless the agreement restricted such a transaction, consider the following possibility: Bob dies unexpectedly and his stock is repurchased by Smith Enterprises for $220.50 per share. Bob's wife would receive $771,750. David and Brett could then elect to sell the company to an acquisition firm for $4,500,000. Granted, this may be a farfetched example, but it underscores the dramatic differences that often exist between the buy/sell price and the fair market value.

Since Bob's 3,500 shares would have been redeemed by the corporation as Treasury shares, the 500 shares owned by David and Brett would represent 100 percent of the outstanding shares.

SUMMARY

There are many ways to value a business. Any of the above approaches could be used to value stock, depending on the purpose of the evaluation. As we'll explore in the next chapter, the value of the stock can also be manipulated through the use of valuation discounts.

Here are some underlying assumptions about valuation of businesses:

1. Assets are appraised, businesses are valued.
2. "Profitable" businesses are worth more.
3. Profitability is determined *after* adjusting for owners salaries, benefits, perks.
4. Earnings power and earnings trends are important.
5. Future earnings are viewed in terms of present value.
6. Assets are discounted.
7. Industry standards and ratios change constantly.
8. Financial statements do *not* accurately reflect value.

12

Valuation Discounts: Manipulating the Value of Your Business

IN 1925 THE U.S. SUPREME COURT RULED, "THE CAPITAL STOCK OF A corporation, its net assets, and its shares of stock are entirely different things . . . the value of one bears no fixed or necessary relation to the value of the other."[1]

Shannon Pratt, a noted valuation expert has written, "All other things being equal, an interest in a business is worth more if it is readily marketable or, conversely, worth less if it is not . . . in many valuations of closely held businesses or business interests, the discount for lack of marketability turns out to be the largest single issue to resolve."[2]

In 1948, the U.S. Tax Court recognized "This is particularly true as to minority interests in a close corporation . . ."[3]

In transferring a family business to children or key employees, the owner's dilemma is often to balance his position as an entrepreneur and his position as a parent.

As an entrepreneur and founder of a company, the business owner wants to realize the highest value possible when he sells or disposes of the company. The sale price establishes the measure of the business's success. The founder's years of effort can all be condensed into negotiations over the sale of the business. During the negotiations, the owner's representatives attempt to secure the highest price possible from the third-party buyer.

The parent/owner knows that the children, or the key employees, cannot compete with large acquisition firms and emotionally recognizes that it will be difficult to get "top dollar" from an internal sale. This parent/owner recognizes that the children or the employees have contributed greatly to the value of the company—through their efforts, their years of service, their loyalty, and their own personal sacrifices.

When selling the business to offspring or key employees, the owner should begin by establishing the fair market value of the business and then applying discounts to the fair market valuation. This method of pricing the business should satisfy the entrepreneurial desire to establish the business value at its highest price; by discounting that price to internal buyers, the owner recognizes their contributions to the business and provides them with an affordable opportunity.

Discounting the price also makes it more efficient for the owner to transfer fractional interests over time. Transferring business interests over time is less costly, both from a tax and cash flow standpoint. The individual shares, valued as a fractional interest, are discounted. The use of discounts can be particularly effective in the elimination or reduction of gift taxes. Therefore, it is less costly, both from a tax and cash flow standpoint.

DISCOUNTS AND PREMIUMS

The previous chapter suggests that the value of an ownership interest in a business could be calculated simply by multiplying the number of shares by the per-share value. In other words, if Mom and Dad own 900 shares of the company, and the son owns 100 shares, then the parents' interest would be worth 90 percent of the total value, and the son's interest would be worth 10 percent. The son's interest is referred to as a "minority interest" and the parents are said to have "control."

As a 10 percent owner, the son only has 10 percent of the vote on business issues, and can be outvoted by Mom and Dad every time. Although he owns 10 percent of the equity of the company and is entitled to 10 percent of all dividends paid, the son effectively has no say in the running of the company. He can voice his opinion, and he may be able to influence his parents' decisions by means other than a formal vote; but Mom and Dad have the legal right to disregard his wishes in the management of the family business. In the extreme, Mom and Dad could fire the son or sell the business out from under him.

Because 10 percent represents a minority interest, an outsider would be unlikely to pay the full 10 percent the son's stock was worth, based on a simple per-share computation. The outsider would probably say, "I'm interested in owning a piece of this successful venture, but I won't pay 10 percent of the total value of the company, when my 10 percent vote is actually ineffective. Instead, I'll pay you 75 percent of what you think it's worth."

The outsider has applied a *discount* to the minority interest he seeks to purchase. Minority discounts upheld in estate and gift tax court cases vary widely,

_____Table 12-1. Minority Discounts_____

*Average discounts for minority interests recognized
by the courts have increased over the years:*

1930 – 1950	17%
1950 – 1970	24%
1970 – 1975	34%

currently averaging approximately 35 percent. As illustrated in Table 12-1, the average discounts for minority interest recognized by the courts have increased over the years.

H. Calvin Coolidge, a former bank trust officer experienced in selling minority interests in closely held companies, presents the following: "A willing buyer contemplating a purchase from a willing seller of a minority interest, being under no compulsion to buy . . . would suffer the same disadvantages of lack of control. The buyer is asked to make an investment with no insurance as to certainty of current yield or as to when, or the amount at which, he may be able to liquidate his investment. Regardless, therefore, of the value of 100 percent of the corporation, the buyer will not purchase a minority interest except at a discount for a proportionate share of the value of 100 percent of the corporation."[4]

Several studies of minority interest discounts have found the average transaction price to be 36 percent to 40 percent below book value.[5]

Note that these discounts were from book value, not from the value of the enterprise as a whole. Assuming the value of the business is in excess of book value, then the surveys would indicate a greater disparity when the minority interest discount is applied to the fair market value of the business instead of its book value.

MARKETABILITY DISCOUNT

Continuing with the preceding hypothetical conversation, suppose Mr. Outsider offers the son 75 percent of what the son feels his 10 percent is worth. While the son contemplates this offer, the outsider explains that the business is not readily marketable. "In fact," says Mr. Outsider, "compared to other investments, it is illiquid. I can't call my broker and just sell the stock. I may not be able to find a buyer when I am ready to sell." Therefore, Mr. Outsider believes his offer for the son's stock should be further discounted for its *lack of marketability*.

In a well-documented study on marketability, J. Michael Maher found that discounts for closely held business interests averaged approximately 35 percent for lack of marketability. Maher's report concludes, "The result is that most appraisers underestimate the proper discount for lack of marketability. The results seem to indicate that this discount should be about 35 percent. Perhaps this makes sense, because by committing funds to restricted common stock, the willing buyer, (1). would be denied the opportunity to take advantage of other investments, and (2). would continue to have his investment at the risk of the business until the shares could be offered to the public or another buyer is found.

''The 35 percent discount would *not* contain elements of a discount for a minority interest because it is measured against the current fair market value of securities actively traded (other minority interests). Consequently, appraisers should also consider a discount for a minority interest in those closely held corporations where a discount is applicable.''[6]

In 1977, the IRS specifically recognized the importance of valuation discounts when it published Revenue Ruling 77-287. The purpose of this ruling was ''to provide information and guidance to taxpayers, Internal Revenue Service personnel, and others concerned with the valuation, for federal tax purposes, of securities that cannot be immediately sold because they are restricted from resale pursuant to federal security laws.''[7]

Referenced in Revenue Ruling 77-287 is a 1977 accounting release by the Securities and Exchange Commissions (SEC), which specifically notes that the discount for lack of marketability can be substantial: ''This reflects the fact that securities which cannot be readily sold in the public marketplace are less valuable than the securities which can be sold . . ..''[8] (See Table 12-2.)

Table 12-2. Marketability Discount: Examples from Court Cases

Case Name	Market Price	IRS Value	Taxpayer Value	Court's Value	Discount from Market
Goldwasser (1944)	82.25	75.88	54.87	68.00	17%
Conroy (1958)	5.00	N/A	1.00—2.00	3.50	30%
Victorson (1962)	.85	.85	—	.50	40%
LeVant (1967)	39.06	39.06	31.50	31.50	19%
Husted (1967)	11.25	11.25	4.20—5.25	7.00	38%
Jacobwitz (1968)	10.00	10.00	1.00	4.50	55%
Alves (1969)	103.00	103.00	77.25	77.25	25%
Bolles (1977)	22.62	15.00	—	12.44	45%
Roth (1977)	2.68	2.00	.75	1.07	60%
Stroupe (1978)	36.00	34.00	6.00	21.00	40%
Wheeler (1978)	5.87	—	2.15	5.29	10%
Kessler (1978)	7.09	4.96	.50	3.67	48%

Note: Marketability discounts are often 35% to 50%.

When a minority interest discount is combined with a marketability discount, the total discount can exceed 50 percent of fair market value for stock transferred to family members.

PREMIUMS FOR CONTROL

In the preceding example, Mr. Outsider discounted the son's interest both for a minority position and a lack of marketability. However, if Mr. Outsider had been talking with Mom and Dad about their 90 percent interest, he might have suggested discounting the price for a lack of marketability. Mom and Dad may counter that their 90 percent should be entitled to a control "premium." The 90 percent stock ownership carries the entire effective voting power of the corporation. Assuming that Mr. Outsider wants to be actively involved in the business, rather than simply an investor, the value of the 90 percent majority interest could actually be *more* than the per-share value. Frequently, control premiums range from 10 percent to 40 percent of the value of the company.[9]

Thus, the value for part of a company does not necessarily equal the pro rata share based on ownership percentage. A minority interest may have only nominal value relative to the total business, while a controlling interest of 75 percent may be worth 90 percent of the total value of the business.

Table 12-3 applies these premiums and discounts to Familyowned Enterprises and revises the values discussed in the preceding chapter.

OTHER TECHNIQUES TO MANIPULATE VALUE

In addition to the application of minority interest and marketability discounts, or premiums for control, other techniques can be utilized to affect value.

The valuation techniques discussed here apply to the value of the business as you know it today. *Prior to* the valuation being conducted, the value can be manipulated by entering into contracts or accruing liabilities that would have a

Table 12-3. Family-owned Enterprises, Inc.; Business Ownership

				Values at 12/31/XX			
Stockholder	# of Shares	% of Shares	Book	Capitaliz. of Gross Revenues	Capitaliz. of Earnings Power	Applying Premiums & Discounts	With Suppl Pension Adopted
Dad	500	50.0%	$200,000	$825,000	$750,000	$1,000,000	$622,000
Mom	400	40.0%	160,000	660,000	600,000	400,000	248,800
Junior	100	10.0%	40,000	165,000	150,000	100,000	62,200
TOTALS	1,000	100.0%	$400,000	$1,650,000	$1,500,000	$1,500,000	$933,000
Per Share Value			$400	$1,650	$1,500	$2000/$1000	$1244/$622

direct impact on the financial statement and strength of the company. For example:

> Dad wants to transfer shares to Son, and is concerned about using book value because of gift tax implications. The capitalization of earnings or an industry standard approach, even after the application of discounts, results in a per-share price that is currently unaffordable. In addition, Dad does not need the dollars to support his personal lifestyle and is willing to defer receipt of part of the purchase price. The price can be reduced further through some additional restructuring. The corporation can recognize Dad's many years of service (for which he may never have been fully compensated) and can provide, on a discretionary basis for Dad alone, a Supplemental Pension Agreement, in addition to any other retirement benefits to which he might be entitled from the company. The company's board meets at its annual meeting and decides to adopt a resolution providing for a supplemental pension to Dad.

Let's assume that Dad is 65 years old, and beginning at normal retirement age of 65, the pension benefit provided by the company is $50,000 per year for 20 years. Although the total payments equal $1 million, the present value is considerably less. The corporation will be expected to provide twenty $50,000 annual payments, which will be reflected as a liability on the company's financial statements. The company's accountants determine that the present value of the transaction is $567,000 the amount the corporation would need to set aside today, assuming 7 percent interest, in order to provide twenty $50,000 payments. At the end of 20 years, the $567,000, plus interest earned, would have been fully paid out to Dad. The present value of $567,000 is a new corporate liability and could reduce the value of the corporation.

After the liability has been booked, Dad begins his stock transfer plans. The valuation discounts discussed previously still apply. The effect here is to reduce the value of the company by $567,000 *before* any discounted stock transfers take place.

SUMMARY

In our firm, we take a number of approaches when valuing the closely held company. Beyond valuing the assets with their earning power, we ask, "What do you need from the business in order to provide a comfortable and secure retirement for yourself so that you won't *need* to sell your business?"

The valuation approach gives us a range of prices to use in transferring the business. Deciding where to peg the price within that range depends on many factors, including requirements for entrepreneurial satisfaction, potential assets for other family members and provisions for a comfortable retirement. As we'll explore in the following chapters, the methods of transferring the business interest can be structured to provide the necessary price and also to minimize unnecessary corporate and personal income and estate taxation as well.

13

Transferring Ownership and Tax Planning

THERE ARE FOUR BASIC STRATEGIES FOR TRANSFERRING OWNERSHIP OF A family business. In the next four chapters, we'll explore these strategies in detail and discuss the variations that accompany these strategies. We'll begin with basic definitions.

1. **Asset Sale.** A sale of business assets by the corporation. Shareholders continue to hold the stock of the company after the asset sale.
2. **Stock Sale.** A sale of the stock of the corporation by the individual stockholders (you); the stockholders no longer own the company after the sale.
3. **Offset Sale.** A sale or transfer of assets or stock which uses qualified and nonqualified plans, along with compensation arrangements to reduce the overall price to the transferee (buyer).
4. **Gifting.** A gift of stock occurs when the donor, during his lifetime, gives away shares to another person without consideration. Although assets may be gifted, it is less common than gifting shares of stock.

Generally, a combination of two or more of the above strategies occurs when the business is transferred. Some type of offset sale usually occurs with an asset, stock, or gifting transfer. The transfer strategy chosen also depends on the configuration of participants who are involved in the transfer.

The list on p. 94 provides an example of a number of different configurations, as well as time frames by which the transfer should be completed.

Transfer Strategy

- Owner → Son or Daughter
- 2 Owners → 2 Active Children, one from each family
- 2 Owners → 1 Active Child
- Owner → Keyman
- Owner → Child & Keyman
- Sale → Outside 3rd Party
- Owner → 2 or More Active Children
- Upstream Planning (Elderly parents still involved as minority or majority shareholders) → "Owner" → Owner's Active Children
- Unrelated Shareholders
- Building Financial Options (No Children, No Keyman)
- Other _____

Timing for Transfer

- Now (ASAP)
- 3 – 5 Years
- 5 – 7 Years

14

Transfer Strategy #1
Asset Sales

THE SHAREHOLDERS OF THE CORPORATION CAN ELECT TO SELL SOME OF THE assets and retain others. Which assets should be transferred? Operating assets, those used in the operation of the business. Which assets should be retained? Those that are not involved in the operation of the business as well as any excess cash, receivables, real estate that may be leased to the new owners, and any other assets not used in the business on a daily basis.

Assume the business is transferred to family members and the new owners form a new corporation. Their new corporation purchases assets from your corporation. The new owners may capitalize their corporation with sufficient cash so that the purchase of assets from your corporation would be an "all cash" deal.

As an alternative, the new owners can still buy assets from your business, but rather than paying cash, they can give you a note for the difference between the sale price and the cash down payment. This installment note is retained by your corporation, which receives interest and principal payments until the note is paid off.

The ownership of your corporation has not changed. What has changed is that your operating assets have been sold to someone else.

The name of your corporation may also be transferred to the new owners, especially if it would be important for the new owners to have it. If the name of your corporation is transferred, then you will have to adopt a new name for your corporation and file it with the corporation commissioner in your state.

Note that *none* of your stock in your corporation has changed hands. If you owned 100 shares prior to the sale of the assets, you will still own 100 shares after the sale of the assets.

Figure 14-1 illustrates the transfer we've described. Prior to the transfer, you own 1,000 shares of Smith Steel Supply, Inc., and receive a salary from the business. The corporation's assets may include the office building and warehouse, business inventory, trucks, and other rolling stock, cash in the bank, receivables, your personnel, and current work in progress.

Assume that you want to transfer your business to your son and you've established the amount of your financial dependency on the business. You want to determine the most efficient way to accomplish the transfer and also satisfy your need for future income. Let's further assume that the real estate in the corporation has appreciated in value since you bought it. Also, you've been able to accumulate cash in the corporation, which is currently in certificates of deposit. Payments for all of the assets of the corporation, including the real estate at current value, and the existing cash represent more than you believe your son can handle. What should you do?

Have your son form a new corporation and capitalize it. His new corporation then enters into a purchase agreement with your company for assets of your company, including the company name. The transferred assets include the rolling stock, inventory, all personnel, work in progress, and finally the name of your business, "Smith Steel Supply."

Your corporation retains the real estate and also the certificates of deposit, as well as the receivables from prior sales. Your corporation enters into a lease with your son's corporation to lease the real estate to him. You may even give him, or give his corporation, an option to purchase the real estate after the installment note for the assets has been paid off.

FINANCING THE ASSET PURCHASE

Your son's purchase of the assets from your business may be financed in one of two ways.

1. Your son goes to the local banker, who is happy to see your family business continue in the community and is eager to establish a banking relationship with your son. The bank provides your son's new corporation a loan to acquire the assets from your corporation; furthermore, the bank extends your son's company a working capital loan to meet payroll costs until such time as sufficient revenues come into his corporation. The Asset Purchase loan and the Working Capital loan are then repaid by your son's corporation to the bank. This arrangement has two advantages: Your son can "cash you out" by providing cash for the assets purchased.

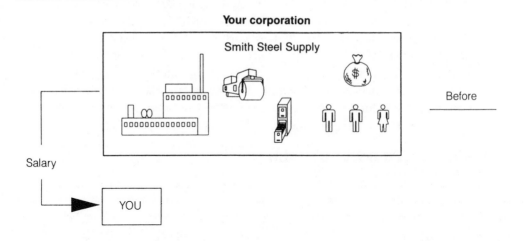

Your ownership is evidenced by the shares you own. For example: 100 shares of Smith Steel Supply, Inc.

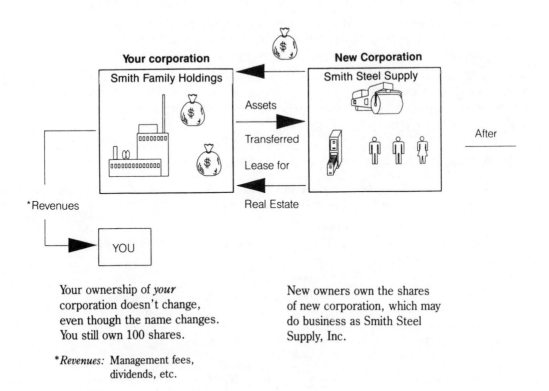

Your ownership of *your* corporation doesn't change, even though the name changes. You still own 100 shares.

*Revenues: Management fees, dividends, etc.

New owners own the shares of new corporation, which may do business as Smith Steel Supply, Inc.

Fig. 14-1. Illustrated example of an asset sale.

Second, your son builds a banking relationship and establishes his identity in the community as a new business owner.

2. With the second financing option, your corporation acts as the bank. Your company sells the assets to your son's company in exchange for a note from his corporation. You might also provide your son the working capital loan so he can meet payroll costs for his personnel. His note with your corporation is amortized over a period of years and, with the rent he pays to use your real estate, provides an income stream to your corporation.

YOUR ROLE AFTER AN ASSET SALE

Your corporation may continue to employ you in your new role as property manager for the real estate assets in the corporation. Your corporate income is derived from collecting previous receivables, rent, payments on the note from your son's corporation, and interest on your corporation's certificates of deposit. You may even decide to make other investments on behalf of your corporation. To the extent that you are actively involved in the business ventures in which you invest, you may be able to draw an ongoing salary from your business.

It may even be possible for your corporation to provide a new retirement plan for you. Your former employees are now working for your son. Your corporation now has only one employee: you. If the income you draw is treated as compensation, you may also be eligible to shelter a portion of the revenues received by your corporation through tax-deductible deposits into a qualified retirement plan for your benefit.

What is important is that your ownership of your corporation has not changed. You still own the original 1,000 shares prior to selling the assets.

In Table 14-1, the transaction and an allocation of the purchase price are outlined, along with a brief summary of the tax treatment of the transaction.

Table 14-1. Smith Steel Supply, Inc.
Allocation of Purchase Price.

	Estimated FMV	Allocation	Tax Treatment
Cash and CD's	$130,000	retained	
Accounts Receivable	70,000	retained	
Inventory	45,000	45,000	Deducted as cost when sold
Land and Buildings	750,000	retained	
Machinery and Equipment	50,000	50,000	Depreciable
Furniture and Fixtures	25,000	25,000	Depreciable
Vehicles	30,000	30,000	Depreciable
	$1,100,000	$150,000	

ALTERNATIVES TO A LIQUIDATION

Effective January 1989, and resulting from the repeal of the General Utilities Doctrine, there are additional tax costs if you decide to liquidate your corporation after an asset sale. Gain from the sale of assets, including recapture of accelerated methods of depreciation, could be taxed at a maximum corporate rate of 39 percent. After the liquidation, the value of the shares in excess of your basis will be taxed to you again a second time.

Therefore, to the extent that you can maintain your corporation and continue to provide services to it, you may be able to draw the income out as compensation. As another alternative to liquidation, your corporation can declare dividends to shareholders; however, dividends also experience double taxation, since they are paid with after-tax corporate dollars and taxed again as income to the recipient.

A third alternative to a liquidation is to contribute your shares (after the sale of assets) to a Wealth Accumulation Trust. You receive tax deductions by putting your shares in the Wealth Accumulation Trust; the Trust can liquidate the corporation, and although the corporation will pay income tax on the liquidation, the Trust can provide you (and your spouse) with a partially tax-free income for the rest of your lives. Wealth Accumulation Trusts are explored in greater detail in Chapter 22.

REAL ESTATE IN THE CORPORATION

The real estate may still remain inside your corporation after an asset sale. You may want to provide your son or his corporation an ability to purchase the real estate at some future date. For example, if you entered into a 10-year lease with your son for the use of the property, you might provide a purchase option to dovetail into the expiration of the lease. Or you might want to give him an option to purchase the real estate sooner, say in five years.

You may want to give your son an option to purchase the real estate at its current value today. Or, perhaps you will want to have it appraised at the end of the lease. Then, the purchase option would allow him to buy it at its then attained value, as determined by an appraiser at that time. You may also want to consider financing this transaction.

Generally, the lease agreement will be a "triple net" lease, requiring your son's corporation to pay taxes, insurance, and maintenance costs. You may even want to have him make any necessary capital improvements to the property. In this case, it would be fair for you to allow him to deduct the capital improvements that he has made during the term of the lease from the price he pays you for the property when he acquires it.

Depending on the timing of your income needs, you may decide to have the asset sale amortized over 10 years. After the installment note for the assets is paid off, you could then enter into a 10- or 15-year note for the sale of the real estate. This allows you to spread the receipt of income from the sale of corporate assets over a 20- or 25-year period. And it provides an attractive retirement benefit, in addition to other retirement assets you might receive from benefit plans.

LIABILITIES OF THE SELLER

In an asset sale, any corporate liabilities that you have would usually remain with your corporation. Sometimes there are specific liabilities, such as mortgages, that the purchaser acquires as part of the transaction. If the purchaser acquires rolling stock, any notes tied to the vehicles usually go with the buyer.

One of the disadvantages of an asset sale is the potential for future lawsuits, which can still be brought against you as the owner of your corporation. Although indemnifications, representations, and warranties may protect the buyer and seller, they won't stop someone from suing you.

TAX TREATMENT OF DIFFERENT KINDS OF ASSETS

In an asset sale, *goodwill* represents the excess purchase price over the value of the assets. Goodwill can neither be deducted nor depreciated by the purchaser, although it does become part of basis. In the event that your son sells the assets to someone else, goodwill is added to basis and results in less capital gain for him. Generally, the buyer would want to allocate as little as possible to goodwill.

Recapture involves taxable income to the seller when accelerated methods of depreciation have been used, rather than straight-line depreciation methods. On sale of those assets, the ''excess'' depreciation is ''recaptured'' as ordinary income by your corporation and treated as ordinary income for corporate income tax purposes in the year of the asset sale.

CASE STUDY

A look at the preceding information as applied to specific situations is illustrative: Let's say you've sold your operating assets for cash to a newly formed corporation owned by your son. Additional consideration was in a noncompetition agreement between you, personally, and your son's corporation. Your son's corporation is paying $75,000 a year to your corporation as rent for the use of your real estate. You're earning another $25,000 per year in interest on corporate cash, which has been invested in certificates of deposit. There's no debt on the corporate real estate, so the $100,000 flowing into your corporation is taxable income.

Your accountant has agreed that at your age, 60, it's appropriate for your corporation to pay you a $30,000 salary from your corporation for property management. The $30,000 is paid from the $100,000 the corporation receives as income.

Since you can live on the noncompete payments you are receiving from your son's corporation, plus the $30,000 salary, you want to defer, on a pretax basis if possible, the receipt of some of the funds and let them accumulate so you can draw on them in later years.

After the sale of its assets, your corporation therefore establishes a new defined benefit pension plan for you. The plan is designed to recognize your past years of service. The required contribution, as determined by the actuary, is $70,000 each year for the next 10 years. As the $70,000 is paid from your corporation into the pension trust, your corporation takes a tax deduction for the contribution.

For tax purposes, the receipt of the $100,000 of corporate income is as follows: The corporation paid you a $30,000 salary and made a $70,000 pension contribution for you; therefore, the corporation has no taxable income. The pension trust receives the $70,000 and purchases certificates of deposit; the interest is tax deferred and compounds inside the pension plan.

Assuming the $70,000 earned 9 percent interest each year, by the end of the tenth year, there would be $1,150,000 in the pension trust and you would be 70 years old.

The pension trust could be paid out as a lump sum, an annuity to you for life, or as a joint and survivor annuity that is paid out to you and your spouse for the remainder of your lives. Subject to the new excess accumulations tax described in Chapter 23, the pension funds could be left in the estate and distributed to various family members. The ability to install a new qualified plan may provide an attractive alternative to a corporate liquidation. The pension trust defers taxation while providing tax-free compounding of funds during the period of deferral. (See Fig. 14-2.)

TAX-FREE EXCHANGE

Recently, we took this a step further in a recent transaction for a client, a business owner who sold his assets to a publicly traded corporation and retained the real estate. He entered into a 10-year lease with the acquisition company for the use of the property, installed the pension plan as described above, and provided himself an effective tax minimization tool.

At the end of 10 years, our client believes he will be able to exchange the stock in his corporation for stock in the acquisition company on a tax-free basis. Also, at the end of 10 years, he should have drained all the cash out of his corporation, thereby leaving it with real estate as its only asset.

By effecting a tax-free exchange with a publicly held company, our client will avoid recognizing capital gain treatment on the sale of real estate, and further avoid the double taxation on liquidation of his closely held business.

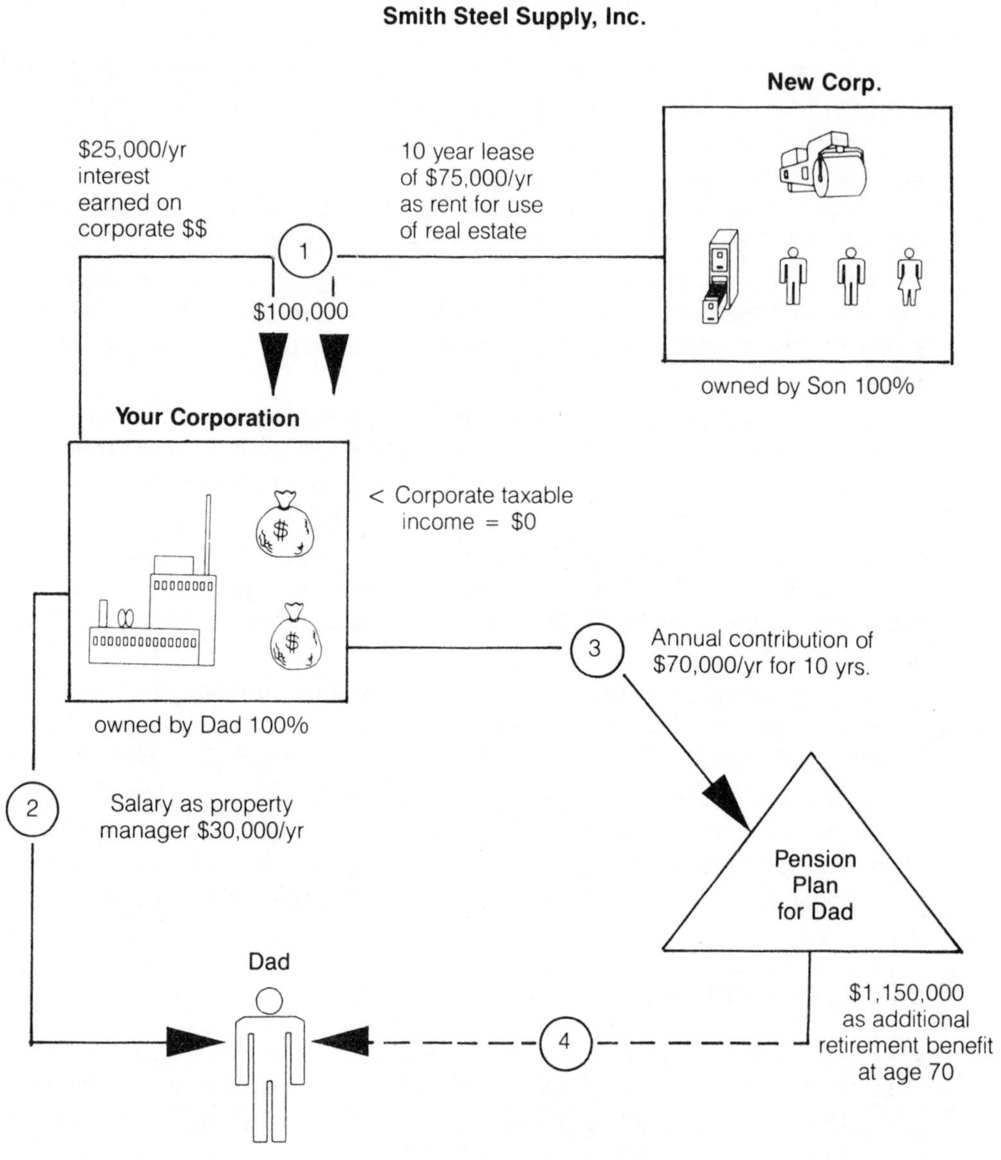

Smith Steel Supply, Inc.

Fig. 14-2. Alternative to liquidation.

The tax-free exchange with the publicly held company works especially well since he will receive unrestricted stock and can sell the stock at any time. Or, he can elect to hold the stock and receive dividends. If he decides to sell the stock, his basis will be the very low basis in the stock of his own closely held company. Therefore, on a sale of stock, almost the entire sale price will be taxable. It will be up to him to decide if, when, and how he wants to sell the stock.

In the event the owner dies with the stock in his estate, the estate will receive a "stepped-up basis" and his spouse could then sell the stock *after* his death with *no capital gain treatment* whatsoever.

As our example illustrates, a number of alternatives are available for someone considering liquidating the closely held business. Tax, pension, and estate implications vary widely, so be sure to consider the impact your decision can have on the future of you and your family.

TAX-FREE SPLIT-OFF

As illustrated in Fig. 14-3, another alternative is to divide the business with a nontaxable transfer called a "split-off." A split-off can be extremely effective when there are multiple locations or branch operations, as well as when there are different divisions or operational components of your business.

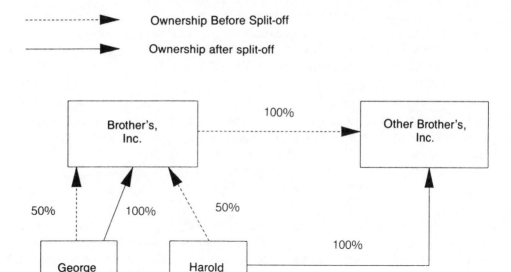

Transaction:

Harold surrenders his stock in Brother's, Inc. in exchange for the stock of Other Brother's, Inc.

Result:

George owns 100% of Brother's, Inc.
Harold owns 100% of Other Brother's, Inc.
Brother's, Inc. owns 0% of Other Brother's, Inc.

Fig. 14-3. Split-off. Nontaxable transfers (non-pro rata).

Consider: George and Harold were brothers as well as model business partners. There has never been any serious friction between the two. Each brother owned 50 percent of the company, and each ran one of the two locations in neighboring cities.

Eventually, the brothers decided to pass their halves of the business to their sons. Though George's location was twice the size of Harold's, the brothers always thought a 50/50 split was fair. The problem was with their sons. Harold's son had been in the business for less than two years; George's son had virtually run his father's larger location for years. George's son protested the 50/50 split adamantly.

The outcome is illustrated in Fig. 14-3. A wholly-owned subsidiary of the parent company was created to hold the assets after the split-off. The assets were allocated to the parent or the subsidiary, and value was placed on each of the assets. Harold surrendered his 50 percent interest in the parent company, and in exchange received 100 percent interest in the subsidiary.

Since the value of the assets in the subsidiary was less than 50 percent of the total value of the business, sufficient cash (or alternatively, a note) was put into the subsidiary so that the value of the subsidiary would equal exactly 50 percent of the business's value prior to the split-off.

The split-off occurred on a tax-free basis and resulted in George owning 100 percent of the parent company, whose value had been reduced by half. Harold owned 100 percent of the now split-off subsidiary, whose value was equal to half of the previous corporation. Harold no longer owned any of the stock in the parent corporation.

This arrangement allowed George to proceed with his son in planning for the parent corporation. Harold could proceed independently with his son in planning for the future of the split-off entity.

The split-off can be especially attractive when there are several successors to the business, and there is concern for a harmonious working relationship. The impact of dividing the business into fractional parts can also have a positive effect on minimizing future estate taxes by creating minority interest shareholders in the resulting split-off corporations. As we learned in the previous chapter, the value of a minority interest in a closely held business may be discounted, resulting in reducing potential estate taxation.

SUMMARY

The asset sale provides a stepped-up basis for the purchaser, allowing him to depreciate the assets as if they were newly purchased. This tax benefit can be an attractive element in an asset transaction.

In addition, by selling certain assets and retaining others, a flow of income can be created to provide future security. At the same time, the transaction can be structured so that it can be easily afforded by the successors.

You can "tax plan" the transaction to defer the receipt of some income and provide supplemental pension benefits for yourself and your family in the future.

The asset-based transaction is common with acquisition companies and should be explored more often in family transfers.

15

Transfer Strategy #2
Transfers of Stock

As WE'VE OUTLINED IN EARLIER CHAPTERS, THE CORPORATE ENTITY IS MORE than the sum of its assets. The corporation is an entity with its own "life," reputation, and value.

Ownership of the corporation is evidenced through the issuance of stock certificates owned by shareholders. The stock certificates represent an increment, or a piece of the total value of the corporate entity.

The value of that incremental piece of the total value doesn't have a specific dollar amount attached to it. Even publicly traded companies find that the price paid for their shares changes daily, based on variables such as the public's perception of the company's performance.

The value of the shares can change, depending on whether they represent a minority interest in the company, or a position of control. Marketability, or the lack of it, also plays a role in the company's value.

The incremental pieces of the company, i.e., shares of stock, can be transferred one at a time or in large blocks.

In this chapter, we'll explore a number of the considerations involved in transferring the individual shares.

TWO TYPES OF TRANSFERS

In most family transfer situations involving stock, there are two objectives to be realized. The first is to transfer a sufficient number of shares to the designated successor, or successors, in order to give them control of the business. The second objective of the current owner is to realize sufficient value to enable the current owner to enjoy financial independence after the transfer is completed.

The transfer of stock to the successor may *not* be the same transaction which creates financial independence for the retiring owner.

LEVERAGED BUY-OUTS

The best buyer for your business is probably right inside your own corporation—that is, your employees or your children.

But employees and family members usually don't have a lot of cash to put down. Because the corporation has value, that collateral can be used in the same way an acquisition firm leverages an asset to create a cash down payment.

A corporation is a revenue stream, a flow of cash through a business. Ultimately, after expenses are paid, earnings or profits remain. Out of those pretax and after-tax cash flows, dollars can be allocated to a seller; employees and family members can buy out the existing owners in much the same way that an acquisition firm operates. In addition, the assets of the corporation may be pledged as collateral until the stock purchase transaction is completed.

Is this transaction any riskier than selling to an outside third party? No. In fact, the family business owner/seller generally has more flexibility because a sale to employees or family members can be arranged all at once or over a period of time. The seller knows his buyer because they've worked together in the business for a number of years. During this time the owner has conveyed operational guidelines and trained his successor for the future.

When the corporation redeems stock from the current owner, payments are generally made by the corporation out of the owner's compensation and fringe benefit costs. Therefore, the cash flow to the corporation is not significantly changed and provides a comfortable income stream to the parent/owners.

IMPACT OF 1986 TAX REFORM ACT

In addition to the perpetuation of the enterprise, one of the primary objectives in transferring a business interest is the removal of the assets from the estate and coordination with overall estate planning. Imagine the surprise of your heirs if, at your death, assets that had been transferred to family members many years earlier are brought back into your estate for estate tax calculations by the IRS. In transferring family business interests, it is important to observe a number of rules in order to avoid the future inclusion of those assets back into the estate.

In the transfer of stock, several new rules resulted from the Tax Reform Act of 1986. They were further clarified in the Revenue Act of 1988 known as TAMRA (Technical and Miscellaneous Revenue Act of 1988) enacted in 1988. TAMRA described how the 1986 law would have a new impact on installment sales, on debt received as the result of transferring a business interest, and on recapitalizations, including voting and nonvoting shares.

Installment Sales

If the sale of your stock to the corporation was treated as an installment sale rather than an all-cash transaction, you will want to avoid having any retained interest in the business, other than as a creditor.

As a creditor, only the principal amount remaining on the note will be included in your estate for estate tax purposes. However, if you are deemed to have a retained interest in the business, the entire value of your stock will be brought back into the estate for estate tax purposes.

Whether an installment sale of the business is treated as a retained interest in the corporation will depend on the nature of the debt. Three rules must be met for the installment sale to be treated as debt: 1. The agreement is entered into at arm's length and for fair market value; 2. The agreement makes no changes in interest in the enterprise; 3. The agreement is not contingent on profits.

Debt

If the debt retained on the transaction by the selling shareholder is "qualified debt" or "start-up debt," the shareholder will not be treated as having retained an interest in the business.

"Qualified debt" means:

1. True indebtedness that unconditionally requires fixed payments not to extend beyond 15 years from the date of issue. This term can be extended to 30 years if the indebtedness is secured by real property.
2. Interest dates and interest rates are fixed or set relative to a specified market rate.
3. The debt is not by its terms subordinated to general creditors.
4. The debt does not grant voting rights or limit others' voting rights.
5. The debt is not convertible into an interest in the enterprise.

To exclude you from having a retained interest in the business, "start-up debt" may also qualify if you loaned funds to other family members to help them acquire a business. As long as your debt isn't convertible into an interest in their enterprise, you don't actively participate in the enterprise, and you don't have voting rights in that enterprise, you have no retained interest in the business.

This can be especially important when you finance a family member who is acquiring assets from your to-be-transferred primary business or is providing services to that business venture.

Recapitalizations

Many business owners have attempted to "freeze" the growth and the value of their business interests in order to lessen the future estate tax liability by recapitalizations or issuing nonvoting classes of stock. The Tax Reform Act of 1986 added an important "anti-freeze" provision through the following:

> "If any person owns directly or indirectly 10 percent or more of the voting power or income stream, or both, of an enterprise and transfers after December 17, 1987, property having a disproportionately large share of the appreciation potential of such person's interest in the enterprise while retaining an interest in the income of, or rights in, the enterprise, retention of the retained interest is treated as a retention of enjoyment of the transferred property for purposes of Code Section 2036(a)."[1]

The above provision means that any property transferred, as well as any interest retained, will be included in your estate.

For purposes of the 10 percent interest in the enterprise test, an individual is treated as owning any interest owned by such individual's family. "Family" includes your spouse; your children; or any children of your spouse; parents; or grandparents; and any of your children's or your parent's spouses.

This provision does not affect transferred property if the transfer was a bonafide sale for an adequate and full consideration in money or money's worth. (See preceding discussion regarding debt.)

The Code does not define what an enterprise is and the Conference Report indicates that enterprise includes "a business or other property which may produce income or gain."

If a parent recapitalizes a corporation into common and preferred stock and gives the common stock to his children, the common stock (as well as the preferred stock) may be included in the parents' estate (unless deemed given away prior to death). The growth interest transferred will be included in the parents' estate. The section, however, does not apply if the typical recapitalization is backwards: that is, the parent retains the common stock and transfers the preferred stock to the children.

Nonvoting Common Stock

The gift (or sale to a family member) of nonvoting stock, combined with the retention of the voting common stock, will also be caught under Section 2036(c). A disproportionately large share of appreciation has been transferred if the potential appreciation attributable to the transferred stock, divided by the value of the transferred stock, is greater than the potential appreciation attributable to the retained stock, divided by the value of the retained stock.

Both the transferred and the retained stock share equally in appreciation potential. However, the voting stock is worth more than the nonvoting stock because of the voting right. When the appreciation potential is divided by the value of the respective voting and nonvoting stock, then a disproportionately large share of appreciation has been given to the transferred nonvoting stock. The nonvoting stock will be brought back into the parents' estate for estate tax computation purposes.

STOCK REDEMPTIONS

A stock redemption occurs when the corporation elects to repurchase from the selling shareholder all of the outstanding shares owned by that individual. The price may be determined by negotiation, by calculation of the individual's need for financial independence, or by other methods, which we've outlined.

The repurchase may be in cash, or it may be paid for over time, as determined by the parties to the transaction.

In Fig. 15-1, the corporation initially issued 100 shares, all owned by the sole shareholder. Over time, the sole shareholder's son came into the business and received, via gift, 10 shares of stock from the sole shareholder's 100 shares. Resulting ownership is as follows: Dad, 90 shares, 90 percent; Son, 10 shares, 10 percent.

Dad now wants to retire, provide for his retirement years, and turn control of the business over to his son. Dad enters into a stock redemption agreement with his corporation whereby the corporation repurchases his 90 shares and retires those 90 shares as treasury stock in the corporation. The 10 shares, owned by the son prior to the redemption, are now *all* the outstanding shares issued by the corporation. The 10 shares represent 100 percent of the outstanding shares.

Dad's transaction was with the corporation and the corporation paid him for the stock. The payment may have been in cash, or it may have been a note. Either will provide Dad with an income stream.

The result is that the son has realized Dad's objective of transferring control and Dad has realized a second objective, achieve value from the transfer of the shares.

Since Dad is now no longer employed by the corporation, the corporation will recover the compensation and benefit costs provided for Dad. The corporation can use those dollars to fund the repurchase obligation to Dad.

BASIS

In the preceding example, you will recognize a gain for income tax purposes on the redemption of shares, which will equal the redemption price paid by the corporation in excess of the price paid by you to acquire your shares (your basis). Your son's basis will "carry over" and will be the basis that you had in acquiring your shares in the corporation.

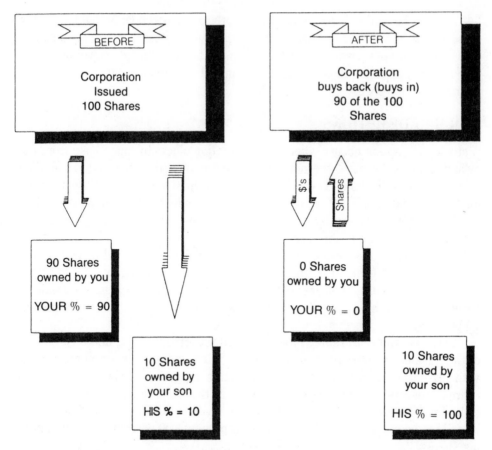

Fig. 15-1. Stock Redemption (individual to corporation). Value is divided into increments (shares of stock).

If basis is an important consideration in the transaction, you may want to consider an outright sale to the individual, rather than a redemption.

DIRECT SALE

A direct sale of stock bypasses the corporation and sells the stock directly to the individual (Fig. 15-2). In this example, the 100 shares that you own are sold directly for the value required to your son or successor. As a result, you have sold all of your shares, your son is the new owner, and his basis in those shares is equal to the price that he has paid. Therefore, if he sells those shares subsequently to a third party, his gain will only be the amount in excess of his purchase price.

You will recognize a gain which will be equal to the price paid by your son or successor in excess of the price that you paid to acquire your shares originally.

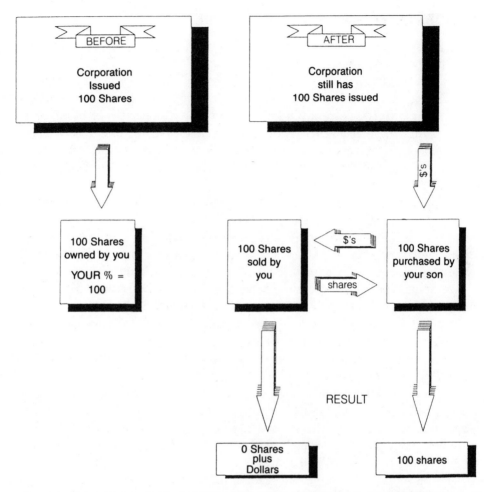

Fig. 15-2. Stock Sale (individual to individual). Value is divided into increments (shares of stock).

The corporation's 100 shares remain issued, as opposed to the previous example when the corporation, after the transaction, only had 10 shares outstanding. In this case, the 100 shares remain outstanding and the obligation is to you from your son or successor for the price of the stock.

Generally, this is not as efficient a transaction, since in order to pay for the stock, your son or successor will have to earn—and be taxed on—those dollars to have them available to pay you for your shares.

Double taxation is often incurred because the corporation increases your son's salary—on which he pays additional tax—so he can pay you for your shares. You pay tax again on the same dollar when he pays you for your shares, since you'll pay tax on the capital gain portion of the shares you transfer to him.

ACCIDENTAL DILUTION OR ENHANCEMENTS

When considering a stock redemption, be careful to avoid an accidental dilution or enhancement of other shareholders' positions.

In the first example, you transferred some of your stock to your son and then the corporation redeemed your shares, leaving your son as the outstanding shareholder with 100 percent. Often, however, a key employee, or other family member, may have received shares throughout the years, either as a bonus arrangement or for various other reasons. When redemption of your shares occurs, the effect of the redemption has an impact on all the shareholders (see Table 15-1).

In the example shown, Dad started the company in 1935, and was originally issued 100 shares. Throughout the years, a key employee provided valuable service, and Dad transferred 10 shares to the employee. In the 1960s, Son joined the business and Dad transferred 40 of his shares to Son. The resulting ownership is seen in the column entitled "Before Stock Redemption."

As you can see, the ownership at that time was that Dad owned 50 percent, Son owned 40 percent, and Key Man owned 10 percent of the company.

Dad died in 1978, and in order to provide income to Dad's wife, his stock was redeemed by the corporation. This arrangement seemed logical at the time, since the corporation had the necessary funds for the redemption and Mom needed an income.

However, one important feature was overlooked. After the redemption occurred, Dad's 50 shares, having been repurchased by the corporation, were no longer outstanding. They became treasury shares. The remaining shareholders were Son and Key Man. Son and Key Man's shares hadn't changed. Son still had 40 shares and Key Man had 10 shares.

Yet those 50 shares represented *all* of the outstanding shares of the corporation, or 100 percent. Son's 40 shares now represented 80 percent of the ownership and Key Man's 10 shares represented 20 percent. Without intending it, the Key Man's ownership in the company had *doubled* through the redemption of the stock.

Table 15-1. Impact of Redemption on Shareholders

Before Stock Redemption			After Stock Redemption		
Shareholder	*No. of Shares*	*%*	*Shareholder*	*No. of Shares*	*%*
Dad	50	50	–	–	–
Son	40	40	Son	40	80
Keyman	10	10	Keyman	10	20
Total Outstanding Shares	100	100%	Total Outstanding Shares	50	100%

As we've explored earlier, having a minority interest in a closely held company has limited value. How will the Key Man realize value from his shares? Without an agreement, what's to prevent the Key Man from transferring his shares to his family members who are not active in the business? Additionally, what's to prevent Key Man's spouse, after the death of Key Man, from demanding dividends for the value of the shares from the company?

If the intent of providing for the employee was an incentive, and the reward was the shares, then a repurchase agreement for those shares *during the lifetime of the employee* should also be provided. Then the employee can be assured that he will be able to realize value from the shares, and the corporation and family members can be assured that they will not be involved with the key employee's spouse or children in the event of death, disability, or termination of the employee.

BUY/SELL AGREEMENTS

Buy/sell agreements are commonly used in family-owned businesses to provide for a liquidation of the interest of a withdrawing or a deceased shareholder when certain events occur. Often retirement is not included as one of these events.

The three types of agreements are as follows:

1. **Repurchase Agreements** (also called entity purchase agreements, or redemption agreements). The issuing corporation buys the interest from the withdrawing party or from the estate of the deceased individual.
2. **Cross-Purchase Agreements.** These agreements are between one or more other individuals or entities. The other individuals or entities buy the interest direct from the withdrawing party or from the estate of the deceased individual.
3. **Hybrid Agreements.** These agreements can provide for either a repurchase by the business or a cross-purchase, in which case the entity and/or the individual shareholders determine at the time the event is triggered who will acquire (business or individuals) the shares being transferred.

Any of these agreements may be either mandatory, or binding, on both parties, or they may be optional on the part of one of the parties to the agreement.

It is not necessary that the provisions in the agreement be applied equally to all the shareholders of a particular entity. If a key employee, a nonfamily member, has an ownership interest, the agreement may provide for a mandatory repurchase when he turns 65, while allowing other shareholders to freely transfer their shares via gift or other means among family members active in the business.

DISABILITY AND TERMINATION PROVISIONS

Often overlooked provisions that should be addressed in these agreements define what will happen in the event of a disability or withdrawal. It is important to provide for disability in the purchase agreement, since the disabled shareholder may have a need for additional income and the value of his shares in the corporation could provide that source of income. When will a disability buy-out occur? What is the definition of disability for purposes of triggering the sale of stock? Will compensation be continued for a disabled shareholder? If so, for how long? What if the disabled shareholder recovers after selling his shares—can he reacquire those shares?

If compensation is continued, the IRS could construe it as a dividend and disallow the deduction to the corporation. A disability salary continuation agreement, however, could provide a continuation of income to a disabled shareholder for a specified period, i.e., until the date at which the disability buy-out would occur. By "dovetailing" these two agreements, income to the disabled shareholder can be maintained, first in a disability salary continuation agreement, and second through the disability buy-out provision regarding the disabled shareholder's stock. A disability salary continuation agreement may be provided for one individual or for a selected group without including all employees.

What happens in the event of withdrawal? Often, voluntary and involuntary withdrawal are overlooked, and in some cases, extra discounts may be applied to a voluntary withdrawal as a method of deterring the shareholder from leaving the company.

Involuntary termination should also be addressed in the agreement. Moral turpitude, felony or criminal charges, loss of various licenses, personal bankruptcy, drug or alcohol abuse—all could cause an involuntary termination and trigger the sale of shares back to the corporation.

Stock purchase agreements should be reviewed periodically to determine if they cover all the important issues, and to determine if the valuation method used in the agreements accurately reflects the underlying value of the corporation.

ATTRIBUTION

Attribution among family members must also be considered and carefully analyzed to avoid unexpected tax consequences to the parties involved in a transfer. Attribution is especially important when considering the estate tax implications of the transfer.

Section 302 of the Internal Revenue Code provides that if a corporation redeems all of the shareholders' shares (so that the shareholders' interest in the corporation is terminated), the amount paid by the corporation to the shareholder or to his estate will be treated as payment in exchange for stock, not as a dividend. In other words, the redemption will be treated as a capital transaction for tax purposes.

The catchphrase is in regard to the corporation redeeming all of the stock "owned by" the estate. In determining what stock is owned by the estate, constructive ownership (or attribution of ownership) rules must be applied. The corporation must redeem not only all of its shares actually owned by the shareholder, but also all of the shares *constructively* owned by the shareholders' family members. One of these rules provides that the shares owned by a beneficiary of an estate will be considered as though they were owned by the shareholder.

For example, assume that Dad owned 250 shares of Corporation's stock, and that his son owns 50 shares. Since Dad constructively owns Son's shares for purposes of the attribution rules, Dad's estate is deemed to own a total of 300 shares. Therefore, redemption of the 250 shares actually owned will be treated, not as a full redemption of stock, but as a partial redemption, and subject under the family attribution rules to dividend treatment.

Under family attribution rules, shares owned by a spouse, children, grandchildren, or parents are deemed to be owned by the shareholder. A full redemption would be eligible for capital gains treatment; a partial redemption will be subject to dividend treatment. In either case, the corporation *cannot* deduct the price paid for the purchase of shares.

Since the Tax Reform Act of 1986 eliminated favorable capital gains treatment and established one maximum tax rate, i.e., 28 percent, the impact of having the transaction viewed as a dividend versus a capital gain has become a moot point. Under current tax law, a capital gain and a dividend are taxed at the same rate to the shareholder. Attribution rules regarding *family attribution* have therefore lost the penalty provisions with the elimination of capital gain treatment. If, however, in the future, capital gains are taxed differently than dividends, this will be an important issue to reconsider.

There are ways to avoid attribution of stock ownership among family members. They are as follows: (1). The shareholder must retain no interest in the corporation except as a creditor, immediately after the redemption; (2). The shareholder cannot acquire any interest within 10 years after the date of redemption; and (3). The shareholder files an agreement (called a *waiver agreement*) to notify the IRS of the redeeming shareholder's acquisition of a forbidden interest within the 10-year period. Although there are additional rules regarding family attribution, the primary issue with the IRS will be to demonstrate that the redeeming shareholder did not have, as one of his principal purposes, the avoidance of federal income tax in the transaction.

SECTION 303 STOCK REDEMPTIONS

Estates comprised largely of close corporation stock may have a liquidity problem in the event of death. Congress enacted Section 303 of the Internal Revenue

Code expressly to aid estates in solving this problem, and to protect small businesses from forced liquidation or merger due to the heavy impact of death taxes. Within the limits of Section 303, corporate surplus can be withdrawn from the corporation free of income tax.

Section 303 provides that, under certain conditions, the corporation can redeem part of a deceased stockholder's shares without the redemption price being treated as a dividend. Instead, the redemption price will be treated as payment in exchange for stock (a capital transaction). Under current tax law, the tax treatment for a capital gain transaction and a dividend are currently the same. The 303 Redemption can safely be used in connection with a partial redemption of stock of a family-owned corporation because it avoids the attribution rules discussed above.

The following conditions must be met if the stock redemption is to qualify for nondividend treatment under Section 303:

1. The stock that is to be redeemed must be includable in the decedent's gross estate for federal estate tax purposes.
2. The value for estate tax purposes of all of the stock of the redeeming corporation, which is includable in the decedent's gross estate, must comprise more than 35 percent of the value of the deceased's adjusted gross estate.
3. The dollar amount that can be paid out by the corporation under Section 303 is limited to an amount equal to the sum of: 1. all estate and inheritance taxes; 2. funeral and administration expenses.

Planning tip. It is important to know that the redemption of stock is normally thought of as a means of providing liquidity to the estate for estate tax purposes. However, there are no requirements that the purchase of the stock by the corporation be in cash. Corporate assets may be paid ''in kind'' as a means of distributing corporate property to the estate. For example, if the objective was to remove real estate held by the corporation from the entity, the value of the real estate could be used to redeem stock from a deceased shareholder's estate. The property would be transferred out, subject to gain at the corporate level. This could be attractive in removing an asset from the corporation which could then be leased back to the entity by the shareholder's spouse, or other family members.

Also important to note is that this must be coordinated with estate planning, since the ability to transfer assets under 303 is limited to the amount of estate taxes due. If the shareholder takes advantage of the unlimited marital deduction provisions in his estate plan, he would eliminate estate taxes, and, therefore, eliminate any possibility of transferring assets out under a 303 redemption.

Always be sure to coordinate your business transfer plans with your estate plans to prevent unnecessary traps from occurring.

16

Transfer Strategy #3
Offset Sales

IF THE DESIRED SALES PRICE IS SUBSTANTIALLY GREATER THAN THE BOOK VALUE of the corporation (or adjusted book value, if real estate is included), then an offset sale should be considered. The actual sale price is based on a stock or asset transfer at a discounted or capitalized earning or adjusted book value. The balance is made up in compensation arrangements or in additional retirement plan benefits. The value of the compensation arrangements or retirement benefits are an "offset" against the total economic value received for the business.

With advance planning (5 to 7 years), a substantial part of the business's value may be "shifted" via a defined benefit plan, nonqualified plan, or supplemental pension plan into an account that benefits the current owners. A consulting agreement or noncompetition agreement or both may complete the offset "package." The resulting transaction—whether an asset sale or a stock redemption—may be more affordable to the buyers because (1). it may be prefunded and (2). a portion may be tax deductible.

Tax deductions to the buyer make the overall transaction more affordable. The deductions provide a method to recover part of the price paid through the tax savings realized by the buyer. The tax savings can range from 15 percent to 34 percent.

The value of the tax savings to the corporation may be an important part of a negotiation. Often the value of the tax savings realized can help to bridge the gap between buyer and seller. Sometimes the value created by the tax savings can allow the buyer to provide the extra dollars that the seller may require to meet standard of living needs, while maintaining the company's ability to pay the seller's "price." If the corporation is in a 34 percent tax bracket, for every $1 that is paid, and deducted, Uncle Sam gives the business a 34-cent refund! For every $1 million paid, and deducted by the buyer, the 34 percent tax bracket business recovers $340,000 in tax savings.

From the standpoint of the seller, there is no difference whether the transaction is deductible or nondeductible to the corporation. Under current law, you'll receive the income in a 28 percent tax bracket in either case. Figure 16-1 shows a hypothetical situation where the "package" is split between a stock redemption and other compensation arrangements which make up the balance.

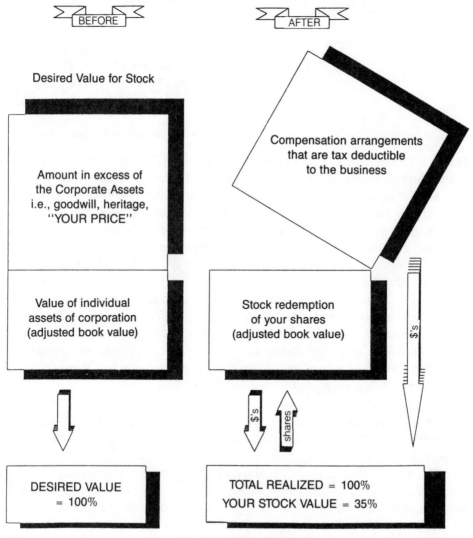

Fig. 16-1. Offset Sale.

COVENANT NOT TO COMPETE

When a business is sold, the parties involved frequently enter into a noncompetition agreement, which restricts the seller or the shareholders employed by the corporation from competing with the purchaser. For tax purposes, an arm's-length payment for a noncompetition covenant is considered ordinary income to the seller and a deductible expense to the buyer, amortized over the term of the noncompete agreement.

The Internal Revenue Service may question whether a portion of the payment made in connection with the sale of the business is separately allocatable to the noncompetition covenant. In addition, the IRS may question the value assigned to a covenant. If successful in arguing that the covenant is a disguised part of the purchase price, the deductibility of payments made by the buyer will be disallowed.

The courts have applied at least four tests to determine whether an amount may be separately allocated to a covenant. The first test focuses on "whether compensation paid for a covenant is separable from the price paid for the goodwill."[1] The second test considers whether the tax effect of the covenant was included as part of the allocatable price in setting the value on the transfer. The third court test questions the existence of a mutual intent by both parties to assign some portion of the purchase price to the covenant not to compete. And the fourth test ascertains whether the covenant is economically real. The courts have ruled that the covenant must have some independent basis or arguable relationship with business reality, such that "reasonable men, genuinely concerned with their economic future, might bargain for such an agreement."[2]

The amount allocated to a covenant should be reasonable and should take into account age of the seller, knowledge of the industry, ability to have a negative impact from the standpoint of competition on the new buyer, and ability to effectively compete, thereby reducing the price or value paid by the buyer.

If the four tests can be met, the noncompetition agreement provides tax deductions to the buyer and a method of compensating the seller for his assurances that he will not compete with the business in the future.

If the IRS contends that amounts paid under the noncompete agreement, or an employment agreement, are disguised payments of the purchase price, the IRS may attempt to disallow the corporate deduction. In litigated cases, the courts have generally respected the treatment by the parties and upheld the payments as representing the contracts that were executed. However, in cases where competition was not a real possibility, or employment services were not intended to be provided, the payments were recharacterized as an additional purchase price. Under current tax law, this does *not* affect the selling shareholder but it does result in a loss of deductions on those payments to the purchaser.[3]

EMPLOYMENT AGREEMENTS

If you plan on remaining active in the business after the transfer of ownership, in order to receive additional compensation in the future, you may want to consider having an employment or consulting agreement. This compensation would be for services provided and would be in excess of the purchase price. (If there are personality conflicts, or if there was hostility involved in the transaction, you probably will not want to be involved in the business after the transfer of ownership.)

The consulting or employment agreement provides for specific duties. Someone else will be running the business; you will be an employee. Your services may be required by the new owners in order to take advantage of your community and industry reputation and relationships. Your willingness and ability to provide expertise and knowledge to the new owners could be an important factor in determining the business's future success.

Keep in mind, however, that any consulting fees or employment contracts in excess of $10,400 (for 1990) will preclude you from receiving any Social Security benefits until you reach age 70. Also, you will be expected to be available to provide services in order for the agreement to meet the Internal Revenue Service requirements and provide a deduction to the corporation.

An *employment agreement* generally is a contract for full-time employment and provides for a continuation of salaries and benefits. If you stay on with the business in some capacity as a full-time employee, the value of the employment contract is usually over and above the value you receive for the business. The compensation you receive for your future efforts on behalf of the business is separate and distinct from the sale price. The sale price represents the value you've created up to a certain point in time. Additional efforts on your behalf should be entitled to additional compensation. Sometimes incentive compensation, contingent on future business results, may be provided as part of the package.

CONSULTING AGREEMENTS

A *consulting agreement* is a philosophically different concept. Your past experience qualifies you to consult with the business on a part-time or "as-needed" basis for a monthly or annual retainer. An issue that will need to be resolved is whether you are an independent contractor, not receiving benefits from the company, or you are an employee entitled to full benefits.

Compensation paid under either an employment agreement or consulting agreement is fully deductible by the company and is received as ordinary income by the seller. Under either an employment or consulting contract, the receipt of funds by the seller prior to age 70 would normally preclude the recipient from receiving Social Security benefits. Therefore, the term of these arrangements should be coordinated with other financial plans to maximize their usefulness.

──────────**Table 16-1. Smith Enterprises, Inc.**──────────
"Offset" Sale

Stock sale:

Cash at Closing	$50,000
Assumption of Existing Debt	25,000
Seller Note, payable monthly at 11% for 10 years	75,000
	$150,000

Noncompete:

Payable $25,000 per year for 5 years	$125,000

Consulting Agreement:

Payable $50,000 per year for 3 years	$150,000
	$425,000

Table 16-1 shows how the transaction of Smith Enterprises and Tom Smith might have been structured with consulting agreements and noncompetition agreements.

17

Using
Retirement Benefits
with an Offset Sale

IT MAY BE POSSIBLE TO PREFUND PART OF THE OWNER'S BUY-OUT BY SETTING aside existing corporate assets or future earnings specifically for the benefit of the owner. Prefunding generally falls in one of three categories: qualified plans, nonqualified plans, or a combination of the two.

QUALIFIED PLANS

Qualified plans are retirement plans approved by the Internal Revenue Service under Section 401 of the Internal Revenue Code. They allow a corporate sponsor to receive a current tax deduction on deposits made and do not tax the recipient until he or she actually receives the funds. During the period the funds are on deposit, earnings on the funds are tax deferred. Recent changes in legislation have tightened rules regarding discrimination and vesting, and the increased restrictions have caused many business owners to terminate or freeze their current retirement plans. This thinking may need to be revisited when considered as part of prefunding a business transfer.

There are two types of qualified plans: Defined Benefit and Defined Contribution. Defined Contribution Plans are generally known as profit sharing plans or money purchase plans. The purposes of our discussion here will focus on Defined Benefit Plans as an offset technique.

DEFINED BENEFIT PLANS

Defined Benefit Plans are designed to provide a monthly retirement benefit when participants reach normal retirement age. The participant, however, has a number of options at retirement age. He can take funds as a lump sum or, alternatively, spread the receipt of funds and receive them as an annuity for the participant's life, or for the participant and the spouse's life.

There are a number of design features that make the defined benefit plan an ideal offset technique, especially if the plan is implemented 5 to 10 years before retirement actually occurs. The benefit provided at retirement is based on years of service as well as compensation. Generally, the owner is the highest-paid employee and has the most years of service in the business.

The maximum benefit that can be provided under a Defined Benefit Plan (for 1990) is approximately $100,000 per year, beginning at age 65 and continuing for the lifetime of the owner and spouse. Alternatively, the maximum lump sum available from a qualified plan without a penalty tax is approximately $1,250,000. Therefore, if no other plans are in place, the lump sum available at age 65 for the owner could be $1,250,000 funded through the defined benefit plan.

A common misconception is that all qualified plans are limited to a maximum corporate deduction of 25 percent of payroll. This limitation *does not apply to* defined benefit plans. The allowable corporate contribution that can be made to a defined benefit plan, and fully deducted by the corporation, is *the amount necessary to fund the benefits* for the participants. Therefore, in some cases, the deductible contribution to the defined benefit plan exceeds 100 percent of the participant's salary.

In Table 17-1 there are six employees in Jamesco, Inc. James, who is 60, owns Jamesco and makes $5,000 a month, while his wife Sue, who is active in the business, makes $1,580 a month. Lewis is a key employee. Three others are participants in a recently established defined benefit plan that requires an annual corporate contribution of $75,894. Of that amount, James receives $60,234 and his wife, Sue, $6,912. Together, James and Sue receive 88 percent of the total corporate contribution. Also note that the contribution equals 100 percent of James' salary while Sue's annual contribution actually exceeds her current salary. The benefit James and Sue are funding is based on their previous compensation, as well as their past years of service to the company.

This plan has been approved by the IRS. The company is allowed to take the current tax deduction for the deposits without taxable income being incurred on the part of any of the participants.

A number of assumptions are made about the defined benefit plan, assumptions that are used to determine the costs of funding the future benefits. These assumptions include interest earned on deposits made, mortality, future salary growth, and the rate of employee turnover. An actuary calculates the number of

Table 17-1. Jamesco, Inc.
Defined Benefit Plan.

Name	Current Monthly Comp.	Projected Monthly Benefit @ Age 65	Lump Sum	Annual Contribution
James	5,000	2,835	$370,637	60,234
			(in 5 years)	
Sue	1,580	550	66,508	6,912
Lewis	2,205	928	96,569	4,745
Bill	1,939	815	84,810	1,687
Bubba	1,591	592	61,604	1,792
Bob	1,021	318	33,091	523
			TOTAL	75,894

James is 60 and will retire at 65. He will be able to withdraw the lump sum amount, roll it into an IRA, or defer the receipt of benefits. The plan provides a benefit equal to 42% of average compensation for those who have been with the company 35 years or more. Those who have less than 35 years of service will receive a reduced benefit. Since the plan is integrated with Social Security, additional benefits are provided for the highly compensated.

---

dollars needed at retirement age to provide the promised benefit to the participant.

Philosophically, this particular design does *not* maximize retirement benefits to rank and file or to other key employees. The plan does attempt to maximize the benefits for those who are most highly compensated and have the greatest number of years of service.

Even if Mom or Dad intend to "retire" in the next four or five years, it is possible to install a defined benefit plan by requiring the next generation to continue funding the plan. If Mom or Dad continue to work at least 500 hours per year for the company, they can continue to receive contributions.

One advantage of the defined benefit plan is its ability to "freeze" the value of the company. In Fig. 17-1, you'll see that without a pension plan, retained earnings in the company are expected to grow over a 10-year period. Assuming that Dad wants to transfer his stock in 10 years, the company or the family members' purchase of the stock at that time can be more expensive; Dad's, or the family's, efforts during that period have resulted in an increase in the corporation's value. The value of the company will have grown, the retained earnings will be greater, and the buy-out of Dad will be more expensive.

By installing the pension plan now, retained earnings can be shifted from the company to the pension trust and may help to keep the earnings of the company relatively flat for the 10-year period, even as those earnings grow inside the pension trust on a tax-free basis.

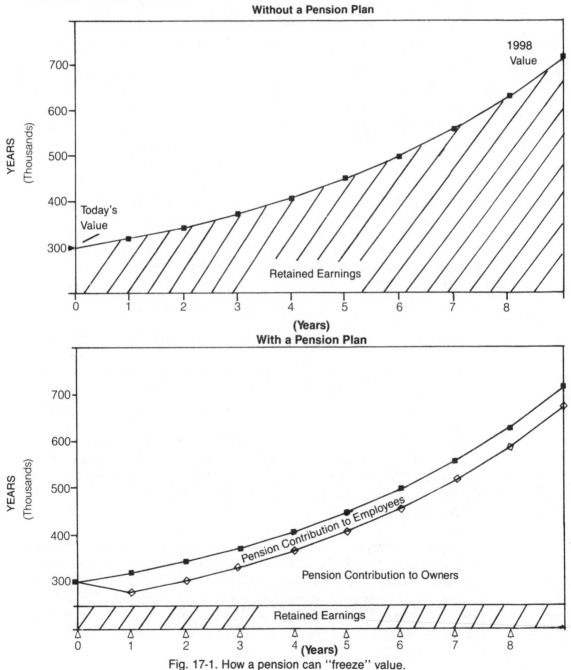

Fig. 17-1. How a pension can "freeze" value.

Retained earnings remain relatively level so that the buy-out of Dad in 10 years will be at approximately the same price as it would be today. The profits of the company have been shifted into the pension plan, mostly for Dad's benefit, thus allowing Dad to be more flexible with the redemption of his stock. Or as we'll explore in the next chapter, Dad may be able to gift some of his shares as an "offset" to the increasing benefits he receives from the defined benefit plan.

While the company receives a current tax deduction for setting the funds aside, Dad isn't taxed on the receipt of funds until he actually withdraws them as a retirement benefit. Meanwhile the dollars are growing tax-free inside the pension trust.

COMMON MISCONCEPTIONS

Are you locked into a defined benefit plan? No. The IRS wants to be sure that a retirement plan is established as a permanent benefit plan for all participants. As Fig. 17-2 shows, the plan can be amended in 10 years to a profit sharing plan or a money purchase plan—one that will probably be more favorable to the next generation of managers.

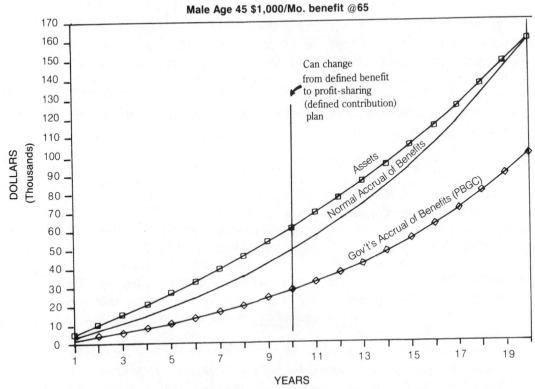

Fig. 17-2. Amending the Defined Benefit Plan.

The plan can be amended to a defined contribution plan without any of the participants losing any of their current benefits. Any excess funds in a defined benefit plan—funds that exceed the amount needed to fund the benefit liability— are allocated to all participants on the basis of their accrued benefits.

Although the use of the defined benefit plan as an offset technique works especially well in companies with fewer than 50 employees, we have used it successfully in companies with as many as 200 employees when there was a dual intent: to set aside funds for Dad, and simultaneously to provide guaranteed retirement benefits for the other employees, especially those with many years of service.

EQUALIZATION WITH INACTIVE CHILDREN

Another feature of the defined benefit plan is its ability to provide benefits with company dollars to children who are not active in the family business. By draining the earnings out of the company over a period of time, Dad can elect to take a minimal distribution for the pension plan beginning at age 70 $1/2$ and conserve the value of the account for his spouse or other children. The amount of Dad's distributions should be calculated to avoid the Excess Accumulations Tax described in Chapter 23.

When there is a desire to shift some of the value of the company to children who are not active in the business, the use of the retirement plan can be especially effective since it allows the shift to occur on a tax-favored basis to the corporation. The retirement plan also provides for tax-free buildup during the period of deferral and can pass as a death benefit to other family members. This may be an effective alternative to having minority shareholders redeem their stock at the death of the owner.

NONQUALIFIED PLANS

The second type of prefunding is the nonqualified plan. Nonqualified plans allow an employer to provide benefits for key employees on a selective basis. Nonqualified plans need not be currently funded by the employer, although there are some practical reasons why these plans are "informally funded." While unfunded plans are exempt from all ERISA requirements, funded plans are subject to ERISA reporting and disclosure requirements, its fiduciary rules, and its enforcement provisions. Therefore, any corporate funds that are set aside are generally in a reserve. The reserve remains a corporate asset at all times and is used only informally to fund the future benefits in the unfunded plan.

Three key areas must be examined when deciding between a qualified and a nonqualified arrangement: the timing of the tax deduction, the tax exemption for earnings on plan assets, and the taxation of benefit distributions. As benefits from unfunded, nonqualified arrangements are exempt from taxation until received, the employer will not be entitled to a tax deduction until the employee is taxed on those benefits.

Refer again to Chapter 9 and Table 9-1, which summarize the difference between qualified and nonqualified plans.

SUPPLEMENTAL PENSION OR SALARY CONTINUATION AGREEMENT

A supplemental pension or salary continuation program is a nonqualified retirement plan that provides several benefits to the corporation, as well as providing a method of funding an offset transaction.

Benefits for the Corporation:

1. Unlike the qualified pension or profit sharing plan, the corporation has complete discretion in choosing the plan participants in a supplemental pension. Therefore, the company dollars can be directed to a select group of one or more key employees.
2. As a nonqualified plan, there are no IRS filing requirements for the supplemental pension.
3. The plan can be designed to provide to the company complete recovery of the full cost of the plan. The recovery provision can reduce the cost of the buy-out.

Benefits to the Participant:

1. The participant in a supplemental pension receives additional benefits that supplement existing qualified retirement plans.
2. Supplemental pension benefits may be received in a year when the participant is in a lower tax bracket, providing tax savings as well as deferrals.
3. The benefits are not subject to the Excess Accumulations Tax, which applies to qualified plan benefits.
4. A preretirement death benefit provided in an amount equal to the retirement benefit would be paid to the family and provide a continued stream of income to a spouse. An example of a supplemental retirement plan is illustrated in Fig. 17-3.

In Fig. 17-3, the company prefunds a $10,000-a-year deposit into a supplemental pension for Dad beginning at his age 55. In 10 years, the company would have set aside $100,000. Assume that the company funds the supplemental pension by acquiring a life insurance policy on Dad. The life insurance policy is owned by, and payable to, the company. The earnings inside the life insurance policy grow tax free. At the end of the 10-year period, the company can elect

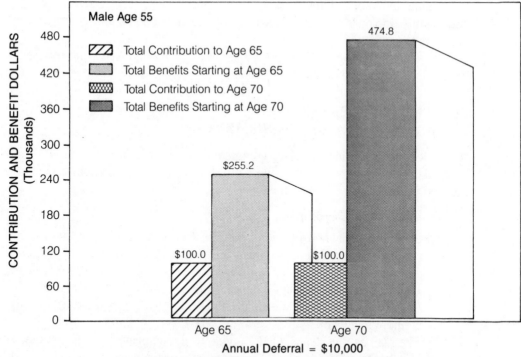

Fig. 17-3. Supplemental Pension Plan. Contribution and benefits.

either to take loans against the policy or pay Dad out of future earnings. Dad's benefit is $25,516 per year for 10 years.

In the event that Dad elected to defer receipt of the benefit until he turns 70 (with no additional company contributions beyond age 65), Dad's benefits are $47,500 each year for 10 years.

In order to pay the benefits, the company may take annual loans against the life insurance policy. The loans are tax-free withdrawals, up to basis, even though the company will receive a tax deduction as it pays the benefits out to Dad. Therefore, in a 20 percent bracket, the company can withdraw $80 from the policy and pay Dad $100. The tax savings to the company make up the difference.

The supplemental pension or salary continuation agreement can be an effective tool in providing Dad with additional retirement funds, while deferring taxation on the receipt of the funds to a later point in time. The tax-free accumulation provides a greater retirement benefit.

The difference between a supplemental pension and salary continuation agreement is that:

1. Supplemental pension can provide benefits at retirement age based on services provided in the past. Properly structured, an individual should be able to receive full Social Security benefits plus the supplemental pension benefits at the same time.
2. Salary continuation provides a continuation of current income instead of providing benefits for services rendered in the past. Salary continuation, if in excess of the Social Security wage limitations, would delay the receipt of Social Security benefits until age 72.

SUMMARY

In Fig. 17-4, the offset sale is illustrated in five components. Assume that your financial requirement from the business is estimated to be $2,500,000, and the adjusted book value of the company is $1 million. The stock purchase price is $1 million. An additional $1,500,000 can be provided in an offset arrangement as illustrated. Through a defined benefit plan, $600,000 is funded; another $500,000 is funded through a supplemental pension, $300,000 is provided through a noncompete agreement and $100,000 through a consulting contract.

When transferring stock or assets of the closely held business to family members or to key employees, the offset sale is advantageous to both seller and buyer. Seller receives the necessary dollars, while tax benefits are maximized for the buyers.

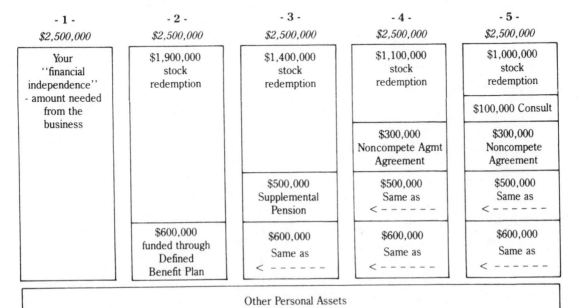

Fig. 17-4. Offset Sale illustrated.

18

Transfer Strategy #4 Gifting the Business

"DON'T GIVE IT TO THEM . . . THEY SHOULD EARN IT," SAID A MICHIGAN OWNER recently.

This chapter will look at gifting business interests to children who are actively working in the business. If you begin a gifting program, you should undertake the program as part of a specific transfer strategy and restrict giving ownership in the business only to those who are working full time for the business.

If you want to provide the same opportunity for children who may enter the business later, your gifting program can have a different timing sequence, contribute the stock to a voting trust (perhaps using some of your unified credit), or provide an option for those children to enter the business at a later date.

BASIC RULES

Our current estate and gift tax laws provide an opportunity for donors to give away $10,000 per donee annually without filing a gift tax return or paying any gift taxes at all. For example, if you have three children, you can give them each $10,000, or $30,000 total. Your spouse can do the same and double the gifting to $60,000. If your three married children each have one child, you can give away $30,000 more. Your spouse can also make a similar gift to each grandchild; all together, you and your spouse could give $180,000 annually to your three children, their three spouses, and your three grandchildren.

Remember: You can give away $10,000 each year; your spouse can give away $10,000 each year; jointly you can give $20,000 each year *per donee*.

You also have an opportunity—either during your lifetime or at your death—to give away up to an additional $600,000 without taxation. Your spouse has the same opportunity. *Jointly* you can make one tax-free transfer of $1,200,000, in addition to the $10,000-per-donee limitation.

Any gifts made in any year in excess of the $10,000 *annual* exclusion will use part of your $600,000 *lifetime* exclusion. For example, if your annual gift to one child (excluding your spouse) was $15,000, $10,000 applies to the annual exclusion and $5,000 of the lifetime exemption is used. You would have $595,000 left. *Although a gift tax return would be filed, no gift tax would be due on this transaction.*

Although many people wait until death to use the $600,000 exclusion, consider using it during your lifetime, especially if the asset to be transferred will appreciate in value. You not only remove $600,000 of value from your estate, but you also remove all the appreciation as well.

VALUE

The value of the gifts should be determined by an outside third party. As we've seen in Chapters 11 and 12, the value of stock in a family business is not a fixed price and depends on many factors.

If you haven't incorporated your business, this may be a good time to consider doing so. A corporate entity allows you to transfer the business in pieces, namely, in shares of stock. Each piece can have its own value, thereby making a transition more easily accomplished over time. You can transfer a number of shares each year until you've accomplished your objective.

In order to "peg" the value for gift purposes, a formula or other method can be used. Sometimes bringing in a key employee as a minority shareholder—with a redemption provision to reacquire his stock when he reaches retirement—can serve to support the value, since it involves an arm's length transaction with a nonfamily member. The formula price established for the repurchase of the key employee's shares can support the value attributed to the shares gifted to family members.

As we've discussed previously, it may be important to use discounts in order to be able to gift more shares in a shorter period. For example, assume the shares have a value of $1,000 per share, and there are 1,000 shares held by the current owner. Total value then is $1,000,000 ($1,000 × 1,000).

Using the annual exclusion of $10,000—and assuming your spouse enters into the gift, you can give $20,000 to your son. You may not want to gift $20,000 to your daughter-in-law, unless you don't object to the daughter-in-law (or son-in-law) owning shares.

Giving $20,000 per year, and assuming the shares remain level at $1,000 per share (which they probably won't), you can only give 20 shares each year. It will take 50 years to complete the gifting!

However, if you recall the discussion in Chapter 12 about lack of marketability discounts, you'll remember we can apply a discount to the transaction. Assuming a 30 percent discount, the gifted shares are now valued at $700 per share. This allows you to gift 28 shares each year, 40 percent more than previously thought. Since it will still take 35 years to complete the gifting, you may want to consider using part of the $600,000 lifetime exclusion to accelerate the process. Table 18-1 and Fig. 18-1 examine the results.

There are some other factors to consider here. Consider this potential catch-22: You are gifting shares to a son (or daughter) active in the business, with the potential to make your business more profitable than it has been. Your gift of stock motivates the son to work harder so that next year when you begin to make another gift, you find that the value of the shares has increased from $1,000 per share to $1,300.

Even applying the discounts, you're faced with the original problem: You can't gift the stock within your desired time frame. What to do?

We've already considered using the $600,000. Let's assume you already used that; what other options do you have?

First, you may want to consider a combination of gifts, combined with a stock redemption by the corporation. The stock redemption could occur now, at your age 60 or 65, at death, or structured in any manner you choose. If, to maintain your standard of living, you will require some economic value for your shares, it may be more efficient to gift a few shares to your active child (or children) and let the corporation redeem the rest.

As we've examined in Chapter 15, be careful of an unintended dilution or enhancement of other shareholder's positions when you use this approach. As an alternative, consider "freezing" the appreciation in the shares by:

1. **A Sub-S election**. Although this involves other decisions, a Sub-S election is effective in freezing value and can shift profits to the individual shareholders, rather than having those profits accumulate inside the company.

2. **A defined benefit pension plan.** This plan could move a substantial amount of the company's earnings into a retirement trust. If the plan design is favorable to the current owners, i.e., most of the contribution is allocated for their benefit, then over a 10-year period, the "profits" of the company could be moved out of the company into the retirement pool. Therefore, if the profits remain flat for this period, there will be little or no appreciation in the value of the stock and the gifting program can be completed. Alternatively, stock can be gifted over five years to a

_____Table 18-1. Gifting Calendar_____

Assume Dad and Mom are planning to retire in 5 years and would like to transfer 49% of their stock to the kids before retirement, without paying any gift tax on the transfers.

Here, Dad and Mom transfer 35% of their ownership right away, using Dad's unified credit, and transfer 28 shares per year using annual gift tax exclusions. The value of the stock is assumed to be $700 per share and remains level.

	Dad & Mom			Kids		
	# Shares	Value	%	# Shares	Value	%
Before gifts	1,000	$700,000	100.0%	0	$0	0.0%
1989 gifts using credit	(350)	($245,000)	−35.0%	350	$245,000	35.0%
	650	$455,000	65.0%	350	$245,000	35.0%
1989 gifts using annual exclusion	(28)	($19,600)	−2.8%	28	$19,600	2.8%
Balance 1989	622	$435,400	62.2%	378	$264,600	37.8%
1990 gifts using annual exclusion	(28)	($19,600)	−2.8%	28	$19,600	2.8%
Balance 1990	594	$415,800	59.4%	406	$284,200	40.6%
1991 gifts using annual exclusion	(28)	($19,600)	−2.8%	28	$19,600	2.8%
Balance 1991	566	$396,200	56.6%	434	$303,800	43.4%
1992 gifts using annual exclusion	(28)	($19,600)	−2.8%	28	$19,600	2,8%
Balance 1992	538	$376,600	53.8%	462	$323,400	46.2%
1993 gifts using annual exclusion	(28)	($19,600)	−2.8%	28	$19,600	2.8%
Balance 1993	510	$357,000	51.0%	490	$343,000	49.0%

currently active child, leaving open the potential for additional gifting to a second child who has not yet decided whether to enter the family business. The gifting program can still be completed within the 10-year period.

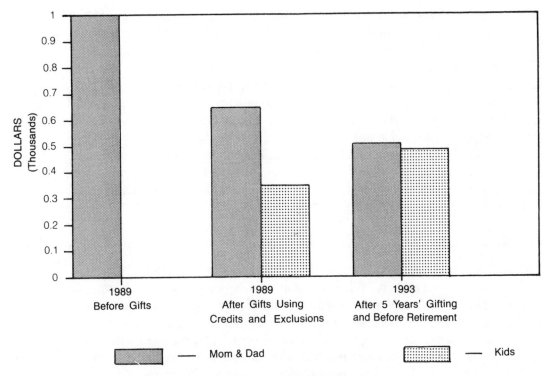

Fig. 18-1. Gifting strategy.

The value of a pension fund can be used to "offset" the buy-out, as we discussed earlier, thereby reducing the cash flow burden imposed on the company if additional dollars for the owner were needed to support his retirement needs.

If the pension account, which, along with other assets, is sufficient to provide for the owner's retirement, then the stock can be gifted to the active children and a stock redemption can be avoided.

3. **Contribute some of your shares to a Wealth Accumulation Trust.** The corporation redeems your shares from the trust, which provides a method of distributing corporate profits. The funds inside the trust can grow tax-free and be distributed as a retirement benefit to Dad and Mom for the remainder of their lives. (See Chapter 22 for a more detailed explanation.)

A NEW OPPORTUNITY FROM TRA 86

Prior to the Tax Reform Act of 1986, the IRS determined that any shares owned by family members—and received as a gift—were attributed to you, the owner, as we discussed in Chapter 15. If you gave some shares away and then had the balance of your shares redeemed by your corporation, the redemption would be treated as a dividend to you instead of a capital gain. Prior to 1986, a complete redemption enjoyed capital gains taxation; a partial redemption was treated as a dividend. Neither transaction was deductible by your corporation, so the tax treatment to the seller had significant and important consequences.

However, now there is no distinction between capital gains treatment and dividends—both are taxed at a 28 percent rate. The issue is moot, *unless* Congress reenacts the favorable provision of capital gain taxation.

The elimination of the attribution problem has created a planning opportunity that will exist as long as dividends and capital gains are taxed in the same manner. Control can be passed to a family member while you simultaneously have the business buy the balance of your stock.

OTHER ISSUES

Although we'll address "equalization" as a separate issue in Chapter 19, some points need to be raised here. When you give a minority interest in the business to someone, are you really giving anything of immediate value? The shares cannot be sold, pledged, or borrowed against, nor do they have real value in terms of an income stream—assuming that *if* you pay dividends, they are nominal. Giving a minority interest provides a mechanism to accomplish a tax-favored transaction at a later date. It does not immediately transfer significant value.

Additionally, the timing of the gifts will need to be addressed, especially if control shifts to the active child. Should the recommended equalization provision in your will and trust (discussed in detail in Chapter 19) value the gift at the date it was made or at the date of death? Valuing it at the date of death may penalize the active child, since any additional value he creates between the time he receives controlling interest and death may be due to his efforts. Valuing the gift for equalization purposes at the date of transfer (before discounts) may be more appropriate.

IS IT GOOD FOR THEM?

Up to now, we've assumed that a gifting program is a viable alternative. Before you enter into a gifting program, however, you'll need to ask whether or not it is preferable for the kids to purchase the shares or work to have the business purchase the shares, rather than receiving them as gifts.

Do gifts have implied strings attached?

Examine how you acquired your shares. If gifting was involved, was it a positive or negative experience? Take a look at your children—are they sufficiently mature? What is their level of commitment to the business?

Examine your own motivation as well. One client frustrated his attorney who consistently recommended he enter a stock gifting program. The client had a seemingly inexhaustible number of reasons why "The time isn't right."

However, when we recommended a sale of stock to the sons, the client immediately responded positively. Unrecognized by everyone, including the client, there was a feeling on the part of the client that, as the founder of the business, he needed to be "bought out" to have a true sense of accomplishment and success. Gifting the stock was objectionable, since it wouldn't give him the satisfaction he desired and received from selling his shares.

Therefore, it's important to understand your own needs and desires, as well as those of your successors, before you enter into a gifting program.

SOME CAUTIONS

Before undertaking a gifting program, consider the following advice:

1. Never, ever give shares without an accompanying stock purchase or buy/sell agreement signed at the same time the gift is made. The agreement can include future gifts, by reference, so the agreement does not have to be reexecuted each time.

2. Consider the possibility of your recipient (your son or daughter) divorcing his or her current spouse. Without a preexisting agreement, the shares may wind up in a divorce settlement, or you may end up with a new minority shareholder!

   Include in a stock purchase agreement an option on the part of the corporation to reacquire shares if a divorce decree is filed. By doing so at the time of the decree, you may avoid having the shares go through the divorce estate and become subject to different interpretations of their value.

3. Consider a "completion clause." What happens if midway through your gifting program you die? The remaining shares would pass through your estate and possibly end in the hands of inactive family members. If a change in control did not occur, i.e., 51 percent of the voting shares, then your active child may be reporting to his inactive brothers and sisters on how to run the business. A "completion clause" protects you and your business by specifying that if death or disability occurs before the completion of the gifting program, the corporation, with a first option, and then the active child or children, have the ability to buy-in, at a predetermined price, all ungifted shares remaining in your ownership.

A SAD STORY

Finally, consider the following true situation.

Mom and Dad worked 40 years to build a successful chain of clothing stores, located in several states. The business had more than 200 employees and $20 million in annual revenue. Two of Mom and Dad's four children had gained experience in retailing and had entered the family business. Dad, who was 65 at the time, agreed to gift the control of the business to the two children during a period of seven years.

Mom and Dad were prudent. They didn't have a lavish lifestyle and only paid themselves sufficient compensation to maintain a moderate standard of living. The business accumulated more than $4 million in cash.

The two sons became impatient with Dad, and two years into the seven-year program, attempted to force Mom and Dad out of the business. Mom and Dad recognized their sons' efforts on behalf of the business and acknowledged it was time to let go. Mom and Dad proposed a stock redemption for the balance of the ungifted shares. Since they had lived so modestly, Mom and Dad required the stock redemption plan to support their needs for a comfortable lifestyle.

The sons, however, refused to pay the price established by an outside valuation firm.

The family was polarized. The two active children sided against the other two children who supported Mom and Dad.

A minority shareholder's suit was threatened and attorneys were employed by all parties. Finally, Mom and Dad voted their stock, regained the control of the company and ousted the two sons.

What began as Mom and Dad's legitimate attempt to create and share the wealth of the business resulted in a divided family and great legal and emotional expenses.

* * * *

Gifting stock of a family business can be a blessing for some and a curse for others. Before you make a decision, understand your motives and protect yourself with contractual agreements in the unlikely event that things go wrong.

19

Equalization

ONE OF THE MOST DIFFICULT ISSUES RELATED TO TRANSFERRING BUSINESS interests arises when one or more children are active in the family business and other children are inactive in the business. The issue is compounded further when the value of the business constitutes the majority of value in the business owner's estate. We've discussed the importance of creating assets outside the business in order to diversify and create value for inactive children. Often that diversification doesn't occur sufficiently for the parents to feel a sense of fairness to their nonactive children.

Although lifetime gifting of stock to an active child can lessen the value of the business in the estate, lifetime gifting can compound the problem of equalization. The dilemma often focuses on how, and from where, additional assets equal in value can be transferred to inactive children. Sometimes the assets transferred are assets that will be important to the parents' retirement needs. Or, transfers do not occur because the parents believe there is no solution to the equalization dilemma. As a result, parents often wind up leaving the business to all the children equally, hoping "the children will work it out."

Timing can confuse the equalization issue further. If stock is transferred to the son today, with the intention to equalize with the other children at some future time, what is the value of the transfer to the son? Is it the value of the stock today? Or is it the value as of the date of the parents' death? If the son or daughter have worked hard to enhance the business's value, why should the value for the inactive children include the increased future value created by the active child?

On the other hand, if the value of the stock transferred today is the value to be transferred to the other children, a timing dilemma exists. The value transferred to the other children may not occur until the death of one or both of the parents.

Therefore, one child may receive stock currently, while the other children will have to wait a number of years before they receive anything of equal value.

Often the value transferred to the active child is a minority interest in the business. As we've discussed earlier, there are severe limitations on the real value of a minority interest. A limited number of shares may not represent any significant value to the active child. Only when control, 51 percent of ownership, passes does true transfer of value occur. Therefore, a minority interest transfer to a family member active in the business should not require an equal transfer of value to inactive family members unless the estate has sufficient assets that can ensure the parents' long-term financial stability. Furthermore, if properly discounted, the value of the minority interest transferred would also reduce the value of other assets transferred to other family members.

If gifting occurs over a period of time, an equalization provision may be included in the will or the trust of the parents, in order to ensure that equalization with inactive family members occurs. Such an equalization provision provides that the value of gifts made to one child during the parents' lifetime will, upon the parents' death, first be made from estate assets to the other inactive family members. This arrangement ensures equal treatment before distribution to *all* family members is made.

In the following example, Mom and Dad have seven children. Three are active in the family business, four are not active. During their lifetimes, Mom and Dad have made substantial gifts of stock in Dad's Manufacturing Company to three of their children, who are active in the business.

Mom and Dad want to be sure that all seven of their children share equally in the total estate. In order to do so, Mom and Dad have an equalization provision in their marital trust agreement. As a result, the remaining four children (those who are not active in the business) will obtain an amount equal to the amount conveyed as gifts during Mom and Dad's lifetimes to the three active children. Upon the death of the surviving parent, the trustee will allocate the remaining trust estate as follows:

"The value of all shares of stock from Dad's Manufacturing Company, which has been gifted to _____, _____, and _____, will be added into the remaining trust estate. The value to be used should be the value of such shares of stock as of the date of transfer to the child.

The total value of the surviving parent's estate, which has increased in accord with the preceding paragraph, is then divided equally so as to provide equal shares to each of the seven children. Each child's share is then decreased by an amount equal to the value of the prior transfer of Dad's Manufacturing Company's stock shares previously gifted to the active child during the parents' lifetime. Such amount remaining as decreased in accord with the preceding provisions is then distributed to the living child.''

An alternative to the timing and equalization dilemma is to gift or sell a few shares to the active child to establish the minority ownership position. A binding stock purchase agreement at fair market value can then be entered into with the corporation. In exchange for a note, the stock would be sold back to the corporation on the death of the owner. The balance remaining on the note could be divided equally at the parents' death among all children. The active children would ''buy'' the business pro rata from each of the inactive children, providing income and fair value to the inactive children while retaining control in the hands of the active participants.

By having the active child or the corporation on behalf of the child buy the stock from the estate, the difficult emotional issues associated with gifting and equalization are eliminated. The transfer is accomplished at fair market value and no favoritism has been shown to one child vis-à-vis another.

As we discussed earlier, if the price the corporation pays on the redemption of stock hurts the corporation's continued existence, a partial transfer of assets in exchange for a note may be a consideration. The subsequent option is to acquire the real estate later, after the asset sale is completed. This arrangement would provide the inactive family members with a source of income from the business, while ultimately assuring the active child or children of their control of the company and its operating real estate.

Other solutions, in addition to those discussed in earlier chapters, include:

1. If gifts of stock are made to inactive family members, repurchase agreements requiring the family to sell their shares back to the company at a certain time (death or retirement of the current owner, for example) also offers value for inactive children. The company can require the children to ''put'' their stock back as a redemption. Making a Sub-S election provides a way to distribute the company's earnings until the redemption occurs.

2. The business can pay for life insurance on the life of the owner, which is ''split-dollared.'' That is, the inactive children are the beneficiaries of the proceeds, and upon death, the business recovers all of the premium it paid. The death benefit is actually ''split'' between the corporation that paid for the coverage and the named beneficiaries. Inactive children receive an income tax-free death benefit and the business is made ''whole,'' since it recovers its cost of funding the program. Or, the death benefit can be used to fund the repurchase of stock held by inactive family members at Dad's or Mom's death.

3. If pension or profit-sharing plan proceeds are available, they can be left at death to inactive children as another equalization provision, as we've discussed previously.

The dilemma of equalization should not be a reason to avoid business continuity planning. If you are committed to the health of your business and any active children involved, then plan your strategy now to provide for children who are not active in the business. Family businesses are often destroyed by factions with opposing interests. With proper planning, you can eliminate potentially warring camps while providing fairly *and* equally to all children.

e years as it has in the past, then they haven't done the critical thinking re-
uired to assume the ownership role.

The written business plan requires this critical thinking and gives the cur-
ent owner an indication of future business operation, an important consideration
o any owner holding a note paid off by future earnings.

The employees' strategic plan needs to address every facet of the business:
its internal environment; its products and services; its organizational structure;
future operations, directions, and goals. The plan addresses the external environment of suppliers, customers, creditors, bankers, markets, and competition.

STRUCTURING THE SALE

If the business is sold to a key group, a leveraged asset purchase is possible.
The ability to sell assets to a new corporation owned by the new owners will
provide you, the seller, flexibility in negotiating price and terms. And it will provide the new owners a new tax basis for the assets.

Refer to Chapters 14 through 17 to review asset transactions, offset sales,
and stock redemptions.

One of the advantages of the asset sale is selling the assets in stages: Stage
one is the sale of operating assets. After operating assets are paid for, stage two
provides for the sale of nonoperating assets like business real estate.

You, as a creditor, are protected because the retention of the real estate,
leased to the new owners during stage one, provides security even if the new
owners fail. By the time the new owners enter stage two, they should be sufficiently established, and there is less risk in transferring the real estate at that
time.

One issue to be negotiated is whether the real estate will be sold to the new
owners (stage two), or retained as an income-producing asset for your family.

Noncompete arrangements and a consulting contract can provide a method
for the new corporation to pay you directly for services, thereby avoiding the
buildup of cash inside your corporation (which you've retained).

USING AN ESOP FOR BUSINESS PERPETUATION

An ESOP (Employee Stock Ownership Plan) is an employee benefit plan designed to purchase stock from the company or its stockholders. The company
establishes a trust fund and makes tax-deductible contributions, up to a maximum of 25 percent of payroll, to the trust, which can then use the money to buy
shares from existing stockholders. Alternatively, the trust can borrow funds
from a lending institution to buy the shares. The company then makes tax-
deductible contributions to the trust to enable the company to repay the loan.

Selling to
Key Person or Group

ASSUME YOU ARE 60 YEARS OLD, HAVE NO CHILDREN ACTIVE IN YOUR BUSINESS, and believe that a sale of the business to an outside third party is your only "out." If you have a core group of key employees who are 15 to 20 years younger than yourself, you may have the ideal "buyer" at hand.

Employees may be more appreciative of the business opportunity than less-than-ready family members, and they may be more willing for you to name the price and terms you want. With employees as buyers, emotional issues of "family" don't cloud the business environment. Secondly, employees tend to be better listeners and become more enculturated in your business philosophies. Third, employees have their own ideas and values, which can help the business grow. And fourth, employees may be willing to make some personal sacrifices to help the "deal" work.

Many current owners make a mistake when they criticize key employees as incapable of assuming ownership responsibilities. Owners overlook one very important fact: the key employee's role as an employee, one who is often excluded from management decisions. Often, employees have valuable ideas that can benefit the business. Sometimes it's the current owner who isn't listening.

THE FIRST REQUIREMENT

The first requirement we impose on a potential employee buy-out is not a financial one. Rather, we require that the employees involved prepare a written business plan. If the employees believe that the business will operate for the next

One of the most important features of an ESOP is the market it creates for shareholder stock.

While the 1984 and 1986 tax law enhanced the attractiveness of ESOPs in several important ways, the 1989 Budget Bill eliminated some attractive ESOP provisions. Preserved, however, are important features:

1. **Tax-free rollover**. If the ESOP owns at least 30 percent of the outstanding shares after the transaction, the proceeds of the sale will not be taxable to the seller if the proceeds are reinvested within 36 months in a domestic security (either bonds, common or preferred stock of a qualifying private or public company) for transactions occurring after July 10, 1989.

   For example, assume you were trying to decide between having your corporation redeem your shares or selling the shares to an ESOP. If you planned to sell $1 million worth of stock, a sale to the corporation would result in a $300,000 tax and you would net about $700,000. A sale to the ESOP would result in $0 tax. You could net the entire $1 million. You actually get about 30 percent more value for your company in an ESOP transaction.

2. **Tax-preferred borrowing**. Fifty percent of the interest earned by a lender to an ESOP may be exempted from income tax. When the lender's savings are shared with the borrower, this can result in a below-market rate. For example, in some cases the interest rate to the ESOP is 80 percent of prime. Both the principal and interest paid on an ESOP loan are tax deductible to the borrower. If you are concerned about being a corporate creditor after the sale of your shares, you can transfer that risk to a lending institution, which provides sufficient funds to the trust and provides you an ''all-cash'' transaction.

   Effective for transactions completed after November 17, 1989, the ESOP must own more than 50 percent of each class of outstanding stock, or more than 50 percent of the total value of all outstanding stock, in order to qualify for the lender interest exclusion. While the low market financing may be attractive, the trade-off of having the ESOP own more than 50 percent of your company may be too high a price to pay for the favorable rate period.

The establishment of an ESOP may indirectly change the way a company is managed. Although an ESOP participant is not a stockholder, the trust is. A board-appointed committee votes the ESOP shares. With the ESOP shares representing a new ownership group, the original owners can no longer run the company for their benefit alone.

Nonleveraged ESOP

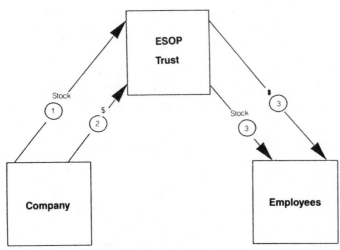

(1) Each year, company gives stock to ESOP or (2) gives cash to ESOP to buy stock. Employees pay nothing. ESOP holds stock for employees and periodically notifies them how much they own and how much it is worth. (3) Employees collect stock or cash when they retire or otherwise leave company according vesting schedule.

Fig. 20-1. The ESOP Transaction.

Leveraged ESOP

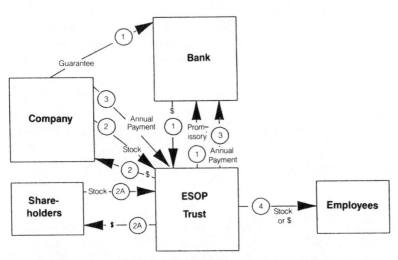

(1) Bank lends money to ESOP with company guarantee. (2) ESOP buys stock from company or (2A) from existing shareholders. (3) Company makes annual tax deductible contributions to ESOP which in turn repays bank. (4) Employees collect stock or cash when they retire or leave company.

The CEO/shareholder may have to decide between no ESOP; and high salaries, perks and benefits, and an ESOP. This means running a tight company and managing it for a higher stock-value growth rate.

The ESOP provides a vehicle for the controlled sale of the business, either gradually or all at once. Ideally, it inspires increased employee loyalty and commitment to the company, as well as higher productivity. Since the allocation of the company contribution is based on compensation, the higher-paid managers usually wind up with the greatest number of company shares.

The ESOP is not for everyone. It is a difficult concept, has a number of limitations, and requires a corporate commitment to fund an increasing repurchase liability as the value of the employees' shares increase. On retirement, the employees can put the shares back to the trust, and the trust must be able to repurchase the shares. The ESOP may be expensive to set up and administer since an annual valuation of the shares must be done by an outside third party.

When an ESOP fits, however, it is a wonderful solution since it creates a ready market for an owner's shares and provides a tax-deductible method of transferring ownership to employees. (See Fig. 20-1.)

SUMMARY

Transferring the business to a core group of loyal managers may be a rewarding experience when there are no family members to help you complete your transfer plans. Selling assets and retaining others may solve your concerns for security and safety; or the employee group may be able to purchase your interests on an all-cash basis, either by leveraging the business assets directly or through the creation of an ESOP to raise capital for the transaction. In either case, an employee buy-out can give you the satisfaction of seeing your business continue in local hands and with people who have helped you build it to its current level of success. (For more information on ESOPs, contact the *ESOP Association*, 1100 17th Street NW, Suite 1207, Washington, DC, 20036.)

21

Creating Options
When You Are Unsure
of Your Successors

WHAT WILL HAPPEN IF PLANS FOR THE TRANSFER OF OWNERSHIP ARE NOT IN place when you die? Who will run the company? Who will own it? Would you want it to be sold? What if the business has been transferred, but other business assets, such as real estate, are owned by inactive family members?

This chapter will address some of the issues that need to be resolved in the event of an untimely death. We'll also discuss the importance of having contractual agreements so that an intended transfer to family members can be completed. If the current owner is waiting for a family member to mature, or to become more responsible, he may postpone the transfer of ownership. If an untimely death occurs and no contracts exist, the children who are working in the business may be deprived of any ownership in the business. The business could be sold to outside third parties, eliminating the family's future employment as well.

Consider this example of verbal agreements. A grandson had been working in the family business for a number of years and had reached a verbal agreement with his grandfather on ownership of the company. It was common knowledge in the company that the grandfather intended to transfer the business to the grandson when the grandfather died. Before the grandfather got around to committing his intentions in writing, he died of a heart attack. Although the aunts and uncles sympathized with the grandson, they pointed out that he didn't have a formal contract with his grandfather. The aunts and uncles overruled the grandson (and his dad) and insisted that the company be sold to the highest bidder in order to realize value for the other members of the family. The grandson was outbid by a large conglomerate and ultimately left the family business.

Often we encounter business owners with only one child. They feel that a testamentary bequest to the son or daughter (i.e., via the will) is an effective way of transferring the business. How wrong they are!

If your will requires that the business be transferred at the first death to the active child, you are probably creating an unnecessary estate tax liability. If the value of the stock being transferred exceeds $600,000, the excess portion will be taxed in the estate. If there is insufficient liquidity in the estate to provide for the payment of taxes, you may be creating an unnecessary burden for the family. Your intentions, of course, were quite the contrary.

Another common response on the part of the owner is to leave the stock in trust for the life of the spouse; after the spouse's death, the stock is distributed to the child. Although this arrangement may eliminate estate taxes on the first death, it can create additional problems on the second death. If the child succeeds in enhancing the business's value, the value of the stock in Mom's estate will be that much greater than the value was on the first death. Since the second estate may not be eligible for the unlimited marital deduction, the estate taxes may be greater on the second death, provided Mom doesn't remarry. You have created inadvertently an incentive for the son to be a mere caretaker, and not an entrepreneur to maintain the company but not expand it.

Any value created by the son for the duration of Mom's life will be partially lost (up to 55 percent) by the higher estate taxes the son will have to pay.

OTHER ISSUES

Additional factors to consider when planning a business transfer include:

- The age and experience of family members
- The role of key, nonfamily employees in the business, both during and after the transition period
- Payment of estate taxes, particularly as they relate to the working capital needs of the business
- The roles of active and inactive family members, and the distribution and equalization of revenues (stock? profits?)
- The business yield
- Income tax implications for distributions made to family members

A number of planning solutions exist. The answers will depend on your willingness to confront and resolve these difficult issues.

DIVERSIFY YOUR ASSETS

The first strategy is to begin to diversify your asset base. If the business value is not the primary asset in your estate, your survivors have the option of keeping the business as an income-producing asset or selling it.

For basic planning, you should maximize your opportunities with qualified retirement plans from the company. Assuming your company is in a 34 percent tax bracket, and you own it 100 percent, *not* having a retirement plan will result in your "owning" 66 cents on every dollar of profit. If a retirement plan results in a company contribution to *your* account in excess of 66 cents on every dollar contributed, then the retirement plan is an efficient vehicle for accumulating personal wealth.

However, if the plan results in your account receiving less than 66 cents on each dollar contributed to the plan, then it's more efficient for you to consider alternative ways of creating wealth.

SUBCHAPTER-S

A second alternative is to consider a Sub-S election for the business for tax purposes. Since the maximum corporate tax bracket is currently 34 percent, and the maximum individual tax bracket is 28 percent, every dollar of profit taxed in your lower bracket saves 6 cents in tax.

For income tax purposes, making a Sub-S election is similar to having your business taxed as a pass-through entity, much like a partnership or proprietorship. All earnings and profits pass through and are taxed to the shareholders pro rata with their ownership.

Earnings and profits can be withdrawn, thereby "freezing" the business value and providing a method of drawing profits from the company that can be used in other ways for personal diversification. Sub-S, however, doesn't perpetuate the business, it merely allows you to withdraw the earnings.

USING A VOTING TRUST

A third transfer strategy is to create a revocable trust and place the stock in the trust. After your death, the successor trustee of the trust would vote the shares. For example, if the family members are not sufficiently mature or experienced to run the business, at death the stock could go into the voting trust. The company could be run by professional managers during the interim period. This will require you to develop a layer of professional management and educate family members on finding and evaluating professional managers who can be hired to run the company. Company board representation should include objective "outsiders" who can maintain continuity, represent the family's interests, and evaluate the professional manager's performance.

In essence, this strategy buys some time. Although a decision may still be made to sell the company, you can evaluate other alternatives without pressuring your spouse to make a premature decision.

During the time it takes the family to gain experience, key employees can be retained by instituting financial incentives based on profitability or earnings of the company. In addition, the supplemental executive retirement plan described earlier can create golden handcuffs to retain those nonfamily key employees during this critical period.

You might also consider transferring a minority interest in the company to those employees with a redemption formula tied to the increased value they bring to the stock while they are running the business on the family's behalf.

COMPLETION CLAUSES

If you've begun a stock transfer plan—whether via gift or sale—to other family members, and you are unsure of their maturity or ability, be sure to have a clause in your stock purchase or buy-sell agreement that gives them an option to buy the remaining interest at fair market value, or to have a first right of refusal if, in the event of your death, your spouse decides to sell the company. The option they would have would be to match an offer from an outside third party. If they are willing and able to do so, it allows the business to remain in the family and eliminates potential disappointments in later years from children who "never had a chance to keep the business in the family."

SUMMARY

Having a contingency plan doesn't mean you've made an irreversible decision. It means that you won't be sorry for decisions you *haven't* made.

22

Making Money by Giving it Away

ROY SOLD HIS BUSINESS TO A LARGE ACQUISITION COMPANY. AS PART OF THE transaction, Roy took back an installment note, which matured in 1990 with a principal amount due of $900,000.

Roy's basis when he sold his stock was very low, so the entire $900,000 would be subject to income tax. The projected tax due was approximately $270,000. With the $630,000 Roy would have left after taxes, he intended to invest in tax-exempt securities and expected a tax-free income of about $45,000 per year for himself and his wife.

Roy wanted to protect the $630,000 for his two children but was surprised to learn that, in his estate tax bracket of 50 percent, another $315,000 in estate taxes would be due after he and his wife died. He was frustrated and angry when he realized that, of the original amount of the note, his family would keep only about 35 cents of each dollar. We suggested that he give the note to a charity.

Roy's reaction was that at least he was keeping $315,000! If he gave it away, he wouldn't even have that. He had already made plenty of charitable gifts while in business. Now he was interested in taking care of himself, his wife, and his kids. "Give it to charity? No thanks."

I asked him to listen to my rationale for giving it away. He agreed. Within an hour, he was on the phone to his attorney instructing him to prepare documents to gift the entire $900,000 note to a local children's hospital.

Here's why.

Roy would contribute the note to a charitable remainder trust, also known as a Wealth Accumulation Trust, but retain an income interest payable for his, and his wife's, life. The hospital will own the remainder interest. The contribution to the trust by Roy qualifies for a charitable contribution deduction. As you'll read in Chapter 24, the present value of the remainder interest can be determined.

In this case, based on IRS tables, the present value of the remainder interest was worth $180,000. This is the amount Roy would take as a charitable contribution deduction on his tax return. The trust is a tax-exempt entity. Therefore, when the installment note was paid off, the trust collected the entire $900,000 and didn't owe one nickel in income taxes.

Point No. 1: In a 28 percent tax bracket, Roy *saved* about $50,000 in income taxes instead of paying $270,000.

Roy has an income interest in the trust and receives all of the income for the rest of his and his wife's life. By investing in high-quality bonds and government securities, the trustee of the trust felt they could achieve a $9^1/_2$ percent yield on the $900,000. Roy's income will be $85,000 per year. After taxes, he will net approximately $60,000.

Point No. 2: Giving the note to charity results in $15,000 *more* annual income than keeping it and investing the net (of tax) proceeds.

Roy had wanted his children to realize some value from the note after both parents die. Roy could use the tax savings he realized from the contribution of the note to fund a "Wealth Replacement Trust."

The wealth replacement trust would be the owner and beneficiary of an insurance policy that would cover both Roy and his wife. This type of life insurance is called a "second-to-die" contract since the insurance company covers two lives in one policy and pays the death benefit on the second death. Since the joint life expectancy for two lives is greater than one life, the cost to acquire this coverage is often substantially less than the cost to acquire coverage on one life.

The properly drafted wealth replacement trust is not subject to estate tax on either Roy's death or his wife's death. The insurance proceeds would be both income tax free and estate tax free to the children.

Point No. 3: The children would receive the full amount of the note, $900,000 on the death of their parents. The $315,000 in potential estate taxes would be eliminated. Roy would gift $8,000 annually to the trust for eight years, so the trust would have sufficient funds to pay the insurance premium. After eight years, no further premium was required. Roy felt he was still ahead in terms of annual cash flow.

Point No. 4: There's a new wing being dedicated at the hospital. Guess who it's named after.

Results of this transaction were: 1. Save over $500,000 in income and estate taxation; 2. preserve a $900,000 asset intact for the next generation, 3. create a

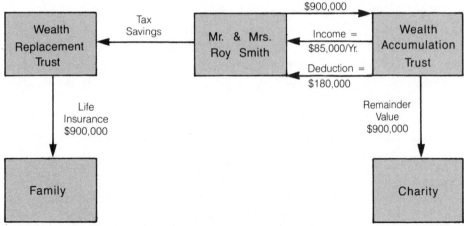

Fig. 22-1. Wealth Accumulation Trust.

new $900,000 gift for charity; and 4. enhance Roy's personal cash flow by 20 percent.

The benefits of charitable giving to solve business transfer problems are unique. Current tax savings can be realized by the donor and appreciated property can be sold by the trust with no tax liability to the donor. Even though the donor and his family benefit, keep in mind the value of the charitable gift and the benefit it will provide.

Now we'll explore several variations on the above.

USING CLOSELY HELD STOCK

Mr. Palmer had voting control of both a corporation and a private foundation. He contributed his stock to the foundation and took a charitable contribution deduction. He then directed the corporation to purchase the shares from the foundation for cash. Neither Mr. Palmer nor the foundation recognized taxable income on the transaction. The IRS argued that, in substance, the corporation had redeemed the shares directly from Palmer (a taxable event), followed by a contribution of the proceeds to the foundation.

The Tax Court supported Mr. Palmer. The IRS lost.

A favorable planning opportunity arises when the donor retains an income interest after transferring stock to a charitable remainder trust. The stock is given to the trust for the ultimate benefit of a qualified charity. The stock should be valued by an outside third party who can substantiate the transaction.

The trust has the right to keep the stock. In actual practice, however, the trustee does not prefer to invest in nonmarketable securities, and the corporation does not want its stock in the hands of outsiders. Therefore, the corporation redeems the stock in a subsequent offer to buy at the established value.

When the stock is placed back in the corporate treasury, a donor who is the sole stockholder has fewer shares but still owns 100 percent of equity in the company. Since the trust uses its cash to provide income for the donor and his spouse, this provides an opportunity to create a future income stream in a tax-favored manner, opening up additional possibilities for transferring ownership to other family members or key employees.

USING REAL ESTATE

The charitable remainder trust can be an effective tool for selling appreciated real estate that has a low cost basis, no debt, and provides little or no income.

Assume that Bill and Sandra have an office building worth $600,000 with a cost basis of $25,000. There's no debt on the building; it nets $24,000, or 4 percent, per year. The charitable remainder trust can sell the building and invest the proceeds at 8 percent to provide Bill and Sandra an income of $48,000 per year.

Bill and Sandra can avoid the tax on selling the building, increase their cash flow, and leave more of an estate to their children if they elect to create the companion wealth replacement trust we discussed earlier.

There are several cautions before making charitable gifts of real property:

1. Have a qualified appraisal.
2. Avoid having a sale of the property already arranged.
3. Accelerated depreciation taken in prior years may result in taxable income to the donor.
4. The property should not be encumbered by a mortgage.
5. Determine if the alternative minimum tax will be a factor.

RETIREMENT PLANNING WITH A TWIST

Nonqualified plans provided by your business for additional retirement income, or as a method of funding an offset sale transaction, are increasing in popularity. Consider using the charitable remainder trust as the vehicle for creating a supplemental income plan that is both nonqualified and separate from the corporate entity. The plan will be "funded," as opposed to the unfunded nonqualified corporate plan, thus providing a method of removing accumulated earnings from the business and sheltering any corporate deposits received from being currently taxable to the employee/participant. Additionally, earnings accumulate on a tax-deferred basis, and the corporation, as the grantor of the trust, gets an immediate tax deduction for the remainder interest.

Key issues, which can be addressed by properly drafting the plan with qualified contingencies, concern potential constructive receipt, economic benefit issues, and forfeiture provisions for the supplemental income plan participants.

As a method of creating a supplemental income and a series of annuity-based deferred compensation payments, this plan represents another method of realizing personal and business goals. This method can help fund the transfer of the family business, or can be used to remove cash from the corporation on a tax-favored basis prior to a sale. By reducing accumulated earnings in the business, the value of the business is reduced, potentially making a sale to family members or key employees more affordable, while creating a lifetime income stream for the seller/parents.

Part III
Estate Planning

23

How Recent Legislation May Affect Your Transfer Plans

MANY BUSINESS OWNERS ARE BLISSFULLY UNAWARE OF THE IMPACT THAT 1986, 1987, and 1988 tax legislation will have on their estate planning. The significance of these recent laws are such that unexpected taxation may occur on either the first or second death, creating an enormous liquidity problem. To satisfy tax liabilities, business interests may have to be sold to outside third parties in order to raise sufficient capital.

Awareness of the changes and planning required to avoid unnecessary taxation is crucial, especially if the business owner wants to keep the business in the family for several generations.

The 55 percent top federal estate, gift, and generations skipping transfer tax rate is now legally frozen. It will remain at 55 percent until 1993, when it is scheduled to drop to 50 percent. Although the top rate of 55 percent is supposed to drop in 1993, current budgetary and economic conditions make this unlikely. In fact, there is a greater probability that the opposite may occur. Rates may be increased, the unified credit may be decreased, or the unlimited marital deduction may be restricted. Any estate over $3 million will ultimately see the assets in excess of $3 million distributed as follows: Uncle Sam, 55 percent; your heirs (jointly), 45 percent. (See Table 23-1.)

Business owners should take advantage of lifetime transfers that are available to reduce estate taxes. Aggressive valuation methods, discounts for minority interest, or lack of marketability may be applied to significantly reduce the value of stock in an estate.

_____Table 23-1. Estate Tax_____

An estate tax is imposed on the transfer of the taxable estate of every decedent who is a citizen or resident of the United States.

The Computation of Tax is as follows:

If the amount with respect to which the tentative tax to be computed is:	*The tentative tax is:*
Not over $10,000	18% of such amount.
Over $10,000 but not over $20,000	$1,800, plus 20% of the excess of such amount over $10,000.
Over $20,000 but not over $40,000	$3,800, plus 22% of the excess of such amount over $20,000.
Over $40,000 but not over $60,000	$8,200, plus 24% of the excess of such amount over $40,000.
Over $60,000 but not over $80,000	$13,000, plus 26% of the excess of such amount over $60,000.
Over $80,000 but not over $100,000	$18,200, plus 28% of the excess of such amount over $80,000
Over $100,000 but not over $150,000	$23,800, plus 30% of the excess of such amount over $100,000.
Over $150,000 but not over $250,000	$38,800, plus 32% of the excess of such amount over $150,000.
Over $250,000 but not over $500,000	$70,800, plus 34% of the excess of such amount over $250,000.
Over $500,000 but not over $750,000	$155,800, plus 37% of the excess of such amount over $500,000.
Over $750,000 but not over $1,000,000	$248,300, plus 39% of the excess of such amount over $750,000.
Over $1,000,000 but not over $1,250,000	$345,800, plus 41% of the excess of such amount over $1,000,000.
Over $1,250,000 but not over $1,500,000	$448,300, plus 43% of the excess of such amount over $1,250,000.
Over $1,500,000 but not over $2,000,000	$555,800, plus 45% of the excess of such amount over $1,500,000.
Over $2,000,000 but not over $2,500,000	$780,800, plus 49% of the excess of such amount over $2,000,000.
Over $2,500,000 but not over $3,000,000	$1,025,800, plus 53% of the excess over $2,500,000.
Over $3,000,000	$1,290,800, plus 55% of the excess over $3,000,000.

Unified Credit against Estate Tax.
   A credit of $192,800 shall be allowed to the estate of every decedent against the tax imposed by the above.

FIVE PERCENT ADD-ON ESTATE TAX

The advantage of the unified credit (currently $192,800) protects up to $600,000 of taxable assets from either an estate or gift tax. Graduated rates, as seen in Table 23-1, actually bring down the average cost of transferring property between generations. Since only a portion of the taxpayer's estate is subject to tax in the top bracket, the effective rate has, in the past, always been less than the top rate imposed on the assets transferred.

For example, on a 1989 taxable transfer of $1 million, the federal gift and estate tax is $345,800. But after applying the unified credit of $192,800, the net tax payable is $153,000. This is a 15.3 percent effective tax rate (15.3 percent × $1 million), even though the asset transferred was in the 34 percent marginal or top tax bracket.

The advantage will be lost if your taxable estate is in excess of $10 million. The true effective tax rate for large estates will now actually be 55 percent of every dollar or asset transferred, due to a 5 percent add-on tax imposed on the amount of the estate between $10 million and $21,040,000. The effect of this 5 percent add-on tax is to create a result the same as if a flat 55 percent rate had been applied to the entire transfer between generations.

The add-on tax becomes increasingly important when considering the impact of inflation or real growth in the value of an estate, therefore increasing its taxability. For example, if the business is worth $3 million today, and its value is increasing at 10 percent per year, then in 20 years, the business will be worth $12 million! Any planning you do today to transfer or freeze future growth in value could potentially save over $4 million in estate taxes! Many 65 year olds live an additional 20 years.

THE GENERATION-SKIPPING TRANSFER TAX

Whenever you make a gift, either directly or in trust to grandchildren, the generation-skipping transfer tax must be considered in addition to any other taxes. A 1988 legal change restricts what was previously a $2 million per grandchild exemption.

When you put property in trust, (my son for life, and then to my grandchild) the generation-skipping transfer tax is not imposed on the value of what is put *into* the trust. Rather the tax is placed on the value of trust assets at the time the skip occurs. Typically, the skip will occur at the death of the child. Therefore, if the property has appreciated during the child's life, the tax will be imposed on the property's value on the child's death *prior* to the receipt of the asset by the grandchild. Clearly, additional planning is necessary if you are considering placing assets in trust for grandchildren.

THE 15 PERCENT EXCESS ACCUMULATIONS TAX

In 1986, a new additional estate tax was created. By not taking a distribution, those who avoided the income tax, payable on distributions from qualified retirement plans, will now be hit with a new "death tax" on the value of excess distributions. The "death time" tax is imposed in addition to any regular estate tax and is equal to 15 percent of the excess retirement accumulation.

In order to estimate the excess accumulations tax, add the amount payable under all qualified pension, profit sharing and other qualified retirement plans, tax deferred annuities, and IRA's. Then subtract an amount equal to the present value of a $150,000 life annuity. Any excess is subject to a flat 15 percent tax.

For example, assume $2 million has accumulated in retirement plans, IRA's, or tax deferred annuities. For a 75-year-old, the present value of a $150,000 annuity payable for life is approximately $1,250,000. Subtracting that amount from $2 million equals $750,000. The excess accumulations tax is $112,500 ($750,000 × 15%). (See Table 23-2.)

Table 23-2. Excess Retirement Accumulations

(Sample Calculation)

1. Determine total accumulation payable: **$2,000,000**
2. Calculate annual protected amount
   ($150,000 or $112,500 indexed): **$150,000**
3. Assumed age at death: **75**
4. Determine discount factor from mortality tables
   (example from 1983 Individual Annuity Mortality): **8.31673**
5. Multiply Step 2 by Step 4 to arrive
   at total protected amount: **$1,250,000**
6. Subtract "protected amount"
   (Step 5) from total accumulations
   to find amount subject to tax: **$750,000**
7. Multiply Step 6 by .15 to determine
   excess accumulations tax: **$112,500**

Careful planning is required so that lifetime distributions taken can draw down the excess portion. If retirement plan assets are not needed for current income, the value of the retirement plan assets could be gifted to the next generation. If the retirement plan assets are being gifted as an equalization provision to children who are not active in the business, the value of the retirement plan assets in excess of $600,000 will be taxed on the transfer, if you used no portion of your unified credit during your lifetime. However, it may be advantageous to take advantage of the graduated gift and estate tax rates by paying taxes on these funds during your lifetime, rather than having them accumulate and remain in your estate. If they were distributed on death, the funds may be at a higher marginal tax rate.

For example, $1 million in retirement assets gifted to your children would result in gift taxes of only $45,500. Assuming no growth, and passing that through the estate to your spouse, could result in the excess accumulations tax plus a higher estate tax on your spouse's death.

Two issues to consider: (1). The timing of the distribution. If Child No. 1 acquires the business, then Child No. 2 could receive assets from retirement plans to equalize; (2). Your spouse's need for income will impact your decision. If the assets are distributed outright to children, the income from those assets will not be available to support your spouse. Planning for spousal income could be arranged through an income interest in an irrevocable trust. The irrevocable trust would remove additional assets from the estate for estate tax purposes while retaining needed income for the spouse. Alternatively, a nonqualified plan could provide income for your spouse as a death benefit.

The excess accumulations tax cannot be reduced by the estate tax marital deduction even *if* the surviving spouse receives the entire accumulation. Nor can it be reduced by a charitable contribution deduction even if the charity receives the entire amount. The liability for the 15 percent tax rests with the estate. The executor may not be able to recover the tax from the beneficiary who receives the property unless your will or state law requires it. Therefore, even if the assets in the retirement plans were sufficiently liquid to pay the excise tax, the executor may be prevented from collecting the assets from the beneficiary if the will makes no provision.

The increasing restrictions on qualified retirement plans may provide more of an incentive to create a nonqualified plan in order to avoid the 15 percent tax. Nonqualified deferred compensation can provide a supplemental retirement benefit as a deductible expense to the business. The plan can also provide income to your spouse in the event of your death.

As we've discussed earlier, the nonqualified plan can be designed to selectively benefit key personnel in the business. If properly designed, the death benefit provided through a nonqualified plan may escape estate taxes, since the benefit provides an income only during the life of the spouse. At the spouse's death, there is no value of the nonqualified plan in the spouse's estate, since the benefit would terminate.

Employers who anticipate an excise tax burden on the executive's estate could also provide ''an excise tax bonus'' to reimburse executives for their future excise tax liabilities. These excise tax bonuses can be structured so that, at the executive's death, the employer can provide sufficient liquidity to the executor to pay the tax. Simultaneously, the employer can be reimbursed the cost of paying the bonus through a properly funded split dollar insurance program.

ANTI-FREEZE PROVISIONS OF SECTION 2036(c)

In 1987, a new rule, known as the "estate anti-freeze provision," was enacted.

An estate freeze is a method by which an individual shifts the future value or wealth from the current generation to a future generation. The attempt is intended to shift the growth or appreciation on that asset and avoid estate tax on the growth and future value of the asset transferred.

Simultaneously, there's an attempt to retain control and income from the asset transferred. The concept of the estate freeze is generally applied to business recapitalizations, an attempt on the part of the transferor to retain control and income while shifting the future growth to another generation.

A recapitalization freeze occurs when you reorganize the capital structure of a corporation. For example, common stock worth X dollars are exchanged for a combination of common and preferred stock of the same value. The previous value is captured in the preferred stock. Then you give or sell the common (growth) stock that has a minimal gift tax value to your children, while retaining the fixed liquidation/redemption value in the preferred (income) stock. The intent is to freeze the value of the preferred so that all future growth is allocated to the common stock owned by the children.

The freeze removes assets from the estate for estate and probate purposes, and it removes growth interests from the reach of creditors. The freeze also provides an incentive for younger family members to remain in the family business and shifts income to other family members, while retaining income from, and control over, the business.

In 1987, Congress amended the Internal Revenue Code of 1986. The ability to freeze assets in the estate has been significantly changed by the following provision: "If a person has a substantial interest in an enterprise and transfers property having a disproportionately large share of the potential appreciation in that enterprise, while retaining a share of the income or rights in the enterprise, the transferred property must be included in the transferor's gross estate at death." This is effective for transfers occurring after December 17, 1987. Although transfers completed by December 17, 1987, are protected from inclusion, it may be possible to inadvertently "undo" a freeze by engaging in a new transaction that falls within the scope of the new statutes.

There are a number of planning solutions that can be applied in spite of the anti-freeze provisions of the recent tax law. For example, a transferred interest would *not* be included in the estate if you retain only qualified debt from the transfer. However, if payments on the debt, received as a result of the transfer, are tied to gross receipts, income, or profits (or similar measures), then the transfer may not qualify as a bona fide sale, and the entire value of the enterprise transferred may be included in the estate.

If you sell the business to family members for full and adequate consideration using qualified debt, but retain the real estate, which is subject to a lease based on gross revenues, you may fall under the restrictive anti-freeze provisions.

Another method to avoid these provisions can be accomplished when assets or business property are acquired as a "split" purchase with family members who will be actively involved in the management of those enterprises. As discussed in an earlier chapter, a loan to a family member may be structured as new business start-up debt. In either case, proper planning should avoid the inclusion of the enterprise's value at the time of death in the deceased's estate.

Alternatively, selling property or other business assets with high appreciation potential to family members and taking back a series of installment notes may be effective if the following rules are followed: The notes require one or more fixed principal payments on specified dates and have a fixed maturity date of no more than 15 years from the date of issue (30 years in the case of real property).

SUMMARY

It is important to readdress your estate planning each time a major piece of legislation is passed by Congress. The impact new tax laws can have on your business can inadvertently upset your transfer plans. The following chapters will address other practical aspects of estate planning that are crucial to the overall concept of transferring the business.

Creative Property Ownership Interests

*Within the parameters imposed by law, one's imagination
sets the bounds of the intricacies of ownership rights.*[1]

SO FAR, WE HAVE EXPLORED VARIOUS WAYS OF VALUING AND TRANSFERRING
business property, whether through actual assets, or through stock certificates
that evidence ownership rights. Our business property discussions have
assumed absolute ownership of property without restrictions.

Property can also be owned subject to a variety of conditions or limitations;
the restrictions may be on use, or there may be conditions restricting the right
to use the property to a specific time duration.

The valuation of property for tax purposes generally assumes unconditional
ownership. The estate tax is a tax on this right to transfer property at death.
The estate tax is based on the value of all property and rights to property pos-
sessed at death or transferred by gift during lifetime.

If you own property subject to a time limitation, you have an ownership right
that is not perpetual or infinite. These restricted rights can be presently valued,
and the limitations can be quantified. If the unrestricted, infinite use of property
has a value of 100 percent, then a restricted, finite use of the same property is
valued at less than 100 percent. By using actuarial tables, it is possible to value
the right to receive a property interest at a specified future time. It is also possible to value the present owner's interest in the property when it is for a specific
period of time.

Time limitations are important in business and estate planning since they offer another dimension to the concept of valuing business interests. If a minority interest can be discounted, what "discounts" would apply to an interest in property that is restricted or exists only for a limited period of time?

The value of 100 percent of the property can be allocated to two pieces: a *life estate*, which represents a specific time period for ownership rights, and a *remainder interest*. A life estate gives the owner the right to possess and derive income from property for the rest of his or her life, at which time the "right" terminates.

The remainder interest is the present right, which may be owned by someone else, to receive the property interest in the future—for example, when the owner of the life estate dies. This "right" in the future to acquire the property can be measured against the life expectancy of the life estate owner, discounted and expressed as a present value. The value of the property would be divided between the life estate owner and the remainder interest owner.

As you can see from Table 24-1, the value of the life estate and the remainder interest changes, depending on the age of the individual who holds the life estate.

SPLIT-OWNERSHIP PURCHASES

Assume your business is expanding and you wish to acquire a new distribution center for $1,000,000. You are concerned about potential estate taxes. You and your son, a vice president in your company, acquire the land and building through what is called a "split-purchase." You are 50 years old. You purchase a life estate and your son acquires a remainder interest. These two interests equal 100 percent of the rights in the property.

Using IRS tables, you would pay $847,430 for the life interest, while your son would pay $152,570 for the remainder interest. (It is important that you do not provide, via gift, the funds your son uses to acquire his remainder interest.) You would be entitled to receive all income from the property for your lifetime.

Your life estate would terminate at your death. The property and any appreciation would *not* be included in your gross estate. The estate tax is on the right to transfer property. Since you have a life estate, you have no right to transfer the property at your death. Your interest in the property ceases. Your son then owns 100 percent of the property. His entire cost would be the $152,570 he paid for the remainder interest.

Assuming your estate is in a 50 percent estate bracket, you've saved over $400,000 in estate taxes *plus* estate taxes on any appreciation that occurred during the time you enjoyed the life interest. Also, if the remainder interest was owned by an inactive family member, it would provide a method for directing corporate income (rents) to other family members, without jeopardizing the day to day operations of the business.

It is becoming increasingly difficult to retain wealth within the family unit. By sharing ownership from the outset with different family members, the split-purchase provides an opportunity to shift assets quickly and inexpensively.

_____Table 24-1. Life Estate, Remainder, and Annuity Interests_____
(Taken from Estate Tax Reg 20.2031-7 and Gift Tax Reg. 25.2512-5)

*Single Life, Unisex, 10 Percent Showing the Percent Worth of
a Life Interest, and of a Remainder Interest*

Age	Life Estate	Remainder	Age	Life Estate	Remainder
0	.97188	.02812	31	.95254	.04746
1	.98988	.01012	32	.94942	.05058
2	.99017	.00983	33	.94608	.05392
3	.99008	.00992	34	.94250	.05750
4	.98981	.01019	35	.93868	.06132
5	.98938	.01062	36	.93460	.06540
6	.98884	.01116	37	.93026	.06974
7	.98822	.01178	38	.92567	.07433
8	.98748	.01252	39	.92083	.07917
9	.98663	.01337	40	.91571	.08429
10	.98565	.01435	41	.91030	.08970
11	.98453	.01547	42	.90457	.09543
12	.98329	.01671	43	.89855	.10145
13	.98198	.01802	44	.89221	.10779
14	.98066	.01934	45	.88558	.11442
15	.97937	.02063	46	.87863	.12137
16	.97815	.02185	47	.87137	.12863
17	.97700	.02300	48	.86374	.13626
18	.97590	.02410	49	.85578	.14422
19	.97480	.02520	50	.84743	.15257
20	.97365	.02635	51	.83874	.16126
21	.97245	.02755	52	.82969	.17031
22	.97120	.02880	53	.82028	.17972
23	.96986	.03014	54	.81054	.18946
24	.96841	.03159	55	.80046	.19954
25	.96678	.03322	56	.79006	.20994
26	.96495	.03505	57	.77931	.22069
27	.96290	.03710	58	.76822	.23178
28	.96062	.03938	59	.75675	.24325
29	.95813	.04187	60	.74491	.25509
30	.95543	.04457	61	.73267	.26733

(continued)

_____Table 24-1. Continued._____

Single Life, Unisex, 10 Percent Showing the Percent Worth of
a Life Interest, and of a Remainder Interest

Age	Life Estate	Remainder	Age	Life Estate	Remainder
62	.72002	.27998	86	.33764	.66236
63	.70696	.29304	87	.32262	.67738
64	.69352	.30648	88	.30859	.69141
65	.67970	.32030	89	.29526	.70474
66	.66551	.33449	90	.28221	.71779
67	.65098	.34902	91	.26955	.73045
68	.63610	.36390	92	.25571	.74229
69	.62086	.37914	93	.24692	.75308
70	.60522	.39478	94	.23728	.76272
71	.58914	.41086	95	.22887	.77113
72	.57261	.42739	96	.22181	.77819
73	.55571	.44429	97	.21550	.78450
74	.53862	.46138	98	.21000	.79000
75	.52149	.47851	99	.20486	.79514
76	.50441	.49559	100	.19975	.80025
77	.48742	.51258	101	.19532	.80468
78	.47049	.52951	102	.19054	.80946
79	.45357	.54643	103	.18437	.81563
80	.43659	.56341	104	.17856	.82144
81	.41967	.58033	105	.16962	.83038
82	.40295	.59705	106	.15488	.84512
83	.38642	.61358	107	.13409	.86591
84	.36998	.63002	108	.10068	.89932
85	.35359	.64641	109	.04545	.95455

EXAMPLE: At age 50, the value of a life interest in a $1 million distribution center =
.84743 × $1,000,000.

25

Trust and Estate Planning

THE TWO MAJOR TYPES OF TRUSTS ARE *TESTAMENTARY* AND *LIVING* (OR *inter vivos*). Testamentary trusts become effective upon death and are created by will. The governing provisions are included in the trustor's will, rather than in a separate trust document. When probate is concluded, property is distributed to the newly created trust, not to the individual heirs.

Living trusts are created during one's lifetime but may continue after death. The advantage of living over testamentary trusts is that the former are not subject to probate, since the trustee, rather than the decedent, is the legal owner of the property. Even if the decedent were also the trustee, there would be no probate, because this trusteeship would be considered an office that would outlive the current occupant. Should a trustee die, a successor trustee then assumes the office: the trusteeship continues uninterrupted.

State laws and the terms of the trust agreement dictate what the trust does and how it will operate. These laws vary from state to state but generally apply various limitations on the powers of the trustee and on the length of time the property can be held in trust. No state will allow a trust to operate indefinitely (except in the cases of charitable or employee trusts).

The person who creates the trust, the trustor, can determine how the trust will operate within the guidelines set up by the state in which the trust will be effective. The trustor determines the purpose of the trust, the amount and type of property it will contain, the length of time it will last, the beneficiaries, how much they will receive, and when they will receive it. The trustor can also specify conditions that a beneficiary must meet in order to receive income or principal from the trust.

REVOCABLE AND IRREVOCABLE TRUSTS

In some states, a living trust is *assumed* to be revocable unless otherwise specified, while in other states a living trust must *expressly be declared* as revocable.

A trustor can always change a revocable trust, either wholly or in part, during the remainder of his life. An irrevocable trust is an irreversible step; neither the trust nor any of its terms can be changed in any way or form—no matter what the reasons.

ADVANTAGES OF IRREVOCABLE TRUSTS

Irrevocable trusts offer two advantages over revocable trusts: income and estate tax savings. A person who sets up an irrevocable trust will not have to pay any income tax on the trust fund's income, provided that:

- The trustor does not receive any of this income
- It is not used to support someone the trustor is already legally obligated to support
- It is not used to discharge the trustor's legal obligations
- It is not accumulated for the trustor or the trustor's spouse
- Certain powers are not returned or transferred to a nonadverse party (friend of family).

In this manner, the trust operates just as the lifetime gift: taxes are avoided by diverting income to low-bracket taxpayers or by creating new taxpayers.

Property in an irrevocable living trust is not taxed in the trustor's gross estate. This may be significant, especially as a means of creating liquidity in an otherwise illiquid estate. If the trust is the owner and beneficiary of an insurance policy on the life of the grantor, grantor's spouse, or jointly (a "second to die" insurance policy), the proceeds will be paid to the trust and should not be included in the grantor's or spouse's estate, if properly drafted and funded.

If the trust provisions permit loans to be made, the funds can be loaned to the estate to pay estate taxes due on either the first or second death.

Any gift tax due is based on the value of the property at the date of the gift. Thus, all appreciation in the value of that property is not taxable in the gross estate. By having multiple beneficiaries of the trust, annual gifts to the trust may qualify for the annual $10,000 exclusion per donee, thereby permitting substantial gifts made over time to avoid any gift tax.

ADVANTAGES OF REVOCABLE TRUSTS

The revocable trust also offers advantages, the principal one being an avoidance of probate. Because property transferred into the trust then belongs to the trustee rather than the trustor, it is not considered part of the estate. If a revocable trust is to be used in order to avoid probate, it must be funded. That is, property must be legally transferred into the ownership of the trustee.

Revocable trusts have other advantages. Trustors can:

- Avoid publicity and interruption of income to family members as the trust continues operating the day following the trustor's death
- Provide for future incapacity of the grantor and thus eliminate the need for a court-controlled conservatorship
- Place property beyond the reach of creditors, in some states

If stock is placed into a revocable trust, that transaction should be coordinated with any stock repurchase agreements.

POUR-OVER TRUSTS

A pour-over trust is a living trust under which a small portion of the trustor's property is held in trust during his lifetime. The remaining property is willed to the trust upon his death. This technique can place the bulk of a trustor's estate outside court jurisdiction, since the property "pours over" into a non-court living trust. A pour-over trust has the additional advantage of keeping the property within the trustor's control during his or her lifetime. To set up the trust, a minimal amount of property, i.e., $100, must be placed within the trust during the trustor's lifetime.

An added advantage is that a non-court trust may easily be moved from state to state if an out-of-state trustee is used. This is not a method for avoiding probate on property moving into the trust.

LIFE INSURANCE TRUSTS

Living trusts in which the property is the ownership of a life insurance policy or in which a trust would be the beneficiary of a life insurance policy are called life insurance trusts. Such trusts provide trustee management over the proceeds of the policy and capitalize on the tax advantages of trust ownership. If carefully written, the *irrevocable* life insurance trust can shelter the proceeds from the insured's gross estate, as well as from the probate estate of the beneficiary, and from the gross estate of the spouse or other contemporary or older-generation donee.

Setting aside the proceeds, the trust also permits income-tax planning for the future earnings of the insurance proceeds. In addition, the trust offers the advantages of property management and flexibility, with respect to the benefits and eventual disposition of the property.

BYPASS TRUSTS

In order to avoid either the double death taxes or the second tax, it is possible to create a trust giving the surviving spouse or beneficiary a lifetime interest; thus, estate taxes can be bypassed at the second death. Bypass trusts are not limited to married persons; they can be used by anyone wishing to leave a beneficial interest in property to any other person.

MARITAL DEDUCTION TRUSTS

As a result of the Economic Recovery Tax Act of 1981, married persons may either give during their lifetime or leave at death an unlimited amount of their assets to the other spouse. The dollar limit and the percentage limitation on marital transfers have been entirely removed.

In order to qualify for the marital deduction, property transferred to a spouse may be left either outright by specific bequests in a will; by having jointly held property pass automatically to the surviving spouse; or by leaving assets in a trust from which the surviving spouse receives all the income, paid at least annually, and has the unrestricted right to control the principal during lifetime or at death (or both if this power is desired).

It may not always be desirable to transfer to the other spouse all the estate of the first spouse to die. Rather, it may be preferable to omit enough of the marital deduction trust to maximize the decedent's exemption equivalent amount ($600,000 in 1987 and thereafter). By using the marital deduction and then the exemption equivalent amount, estate plans may be structured so that the exemptive amount is set aside in a bypass trust. The remaining assets go into a marital trust or outright to the surviving spouse, ensuring that assets held in the bypass trust will not be taxed at either the death of the first or surviving spouse.

QUALIFIED TERMINABLE INTEREST PROPERTY (Q-TIP TRUSTS)

The Q-Tip trust also qualifies for the marital deduction and offers a major advantage in not requiring the ''power of appointment.'' The power of appointment benefits a spouse who would otherwise forfeit the marital deduction tax advantages because of concerns about giving a surviving spouse the freedom to decide who will ultimately inherit the property, e.g., children from a previous marriage. Trusts with a general power of appointment allow the surviving spouse to direct the property to whomever he or she wishes.

The nickname "Q-Tip" derives from tax laws that require qualifications for the marital deduction, e.g., the property left to the survivor must not be a "terminable interest." This manner of marital deduction allowance is called "Qualifying Terminable Interest Property."

In a Q-Tip trust, it must be specified that the surviving spouse will receive all of the annual income and that, during the surviving spouse's lifetime, no one can appoint any part of the property to anyone other than the surviving spouse. An executor must make this election on the decedent spouse's estate tax return. To use this trust with the exempt amount plan, the exempt amount goes into a standard bypass trust so that it won't be taxed at the survivor's death. The balance of the marital property goes into the Q-Tip trust.

In both the bypass and the Q-Tip trust, the decedent spouse can name the remainder beneficiaries upon the surviving spouse's death. The power of appointment trust would be used primarily by a couple wanting the survivor to reassess the estate in order to select or change the beneficiaries.

COMMONLY USED TRUSTS

Type	*Major Identifying Characteristic*
Pour-over trust	A living trust designed to receive property to be "poured over " from the trustor's will via his probate estate.
Life insurance trust	A living trust designed to receive the proceeds of life insurance; sometimes also to own life insurance.
Bypass trust	A trust that gives surviving spouse or beneficiary a lifetime interest, to avoid estate taxes on second death.
Marital deduction trust	A trust that takes advantage of the ERTA marital deduction by placing assets in trust, so that the survivor has control of both income and principal.
Q-Tip trust	A trust, also qualifying for the marital deduction, in which the spouse has rights to income from the trust until his or her death but has no control over the property within the trust.
Charitable trust	A trust that has a charity as its beneficiary.
Support trust	A trust designed to provide the funds necessary to support a beneficiary.
Accumulation trust	A trust that retains, rather than distributes, all the income it earns.

Discretionary trust/ Sprinkling trust	Trusts in which the trustee has the power to retain or pay out the income earned in whatever proportions deemed best.
Spendthrift trust	A trust in which the principal is protected from a beneficiary's creditors.

26

Common Mistakes in Estate Planning

THERE ARE NINE COMMON MISTAKES IN ESTATE PLANNING THAT ARE OFTEN uncovered during a period of transferring the business.

1. **Improperly drafted or nonexistent stock purchase agreements for business interests.** Often there is no agreement at all. Therefore, the fair market value of the business will remain an asset of the estate and will be subject to probate. Without an agreement, there is no guarantee that the intended heirs will actually receive the business. If the stock goes in trust during your spouse's lifetime (and after your death), what happens if the trustee disagrees with the way the children run the business? What if your spouse remarries? What ability do "active" children have to acquire real estate assets that are used in the operation of the business?

2. **Unrealistic shareholder agreement valuations.** In light of recent tax law changes, a fixed stock redemption or buy-sell price may be subject to the anti-freeze provisions because it attempts to indirectly shift a larger proportionate share of the growth to other shareholder/family members while retaining a disproportionate interest in the estate. On the other hand, valuations often don't take advantage of valuation discounts or offset transfer methods. Overinflated valuations may result in either a larger amount of cash required to transfer assets or unnecessary estate taxation.

3. **Leaving stock of the business to all children equally, regardless of the time spent in the business.** Those who are active in the business and those who are not active will have different interests. For example, those who are not active will see the economic value of the business as their primary inheritance. They will want to derive economic value from that asset. If they are not receiving compensation from the business, the value to be derived can only be paid in the form of dividends. This will be directly contrary to the interests of the active children, who often want to retain earnings and profits in the business to help the business grow.

   The payment of dividends to inactive family members is an inefficient way of transferring earnings out of the company. As an alternative, the active children may attempt to buy out the inactive children, but rarely do the two sides agree on value. This often results in the business being sold. The compensation of active family members may be subject to the control of those who are not active. Again, disagreements often arise as to what constitutes ''fair'' compensation.

4. **Gifts not substantiated with third party valuations.** Whether or not a gift tax return has been filed, the ability to substantiate the value is important in order to avoid the inclusion of the previously transferred assets from being brought into the estate for estate tax purposes.

5. **Improper ownership of life insurance.** Although life insurance proceeds are received income tax free by the beneficiary, they are often inadvertently included in the estate for estate tax purposes. Therefore, the insurance policy that is being purchased to provide liquidity to solve an estate problem may be partially causing the actual problem it is designed to solve! Even though received income tax free, if the insurance is included in the estate for estate tax purposes, the insurance may inflate the estate by the amount of proceeds received. Therefore, an additional estate tax will be required, due on the amount of life insurance received.

   Properly structuring the ownership of insurance can remove the value of the policy from the estate. This can result in the policy providing *both* an income and estate tax free benefit.

6. **Having the wrong insurance beneficiary.** Having insurance proceeds paid to the corporation, to a spouse, or to others may also inadvertently include the proceeds in the estate for estate tax purposes. For example, if you retain a 51 percent ownership interest in the business, and the insurance proceeds are paid to the business, then the value of your business interest will increase directly as a result of the cash infusion of the life insurance. Your 51 percent interest in the business will increase, and the value in the estate will also increase.

You may intend to provide insurance for your spouse so that your spouse has an income from the proceeds of the policy during her lifetime. Ultimately, you may intend that the remainder go to the children on the second death. By having the proceeds paid directly to your spouse, the balance of the proceeds not used by your spouse during his or her lifetime will be included in his or her estate for estate tax purposes. An irrevocable life insurance trust as the owner and beneficiary of the insurance avoids this situation.

The irrevocable life insurance trust still provides income to your spouse for her lifetime but eliminates the value of the insurance proceeds in her estate. You could save estate taxes (on the second death) and increase the amount the children will eventually receive as an inheritance.

7. **Not using a Credit or Bypass trust and thereby having the spouse's estate unnecessarily paying taxes on the second death.** There has been a great deal of publicity surrounding the change in the estate tax laws since 1981. With an unlimited marital deduction, many people still do not understand that leaving everything directly to a spouse is not the most efficient way to transfer assets.

The unlimited marital deduction allows you to leave all your assets to your spouse and avoid any estate tax on the transfer. This may not be the wisest thing to do. For example, let's assume that you haven't made any gifts during your lifetime. At death, you transfer $600,000 in assets to your son with the balance going to your spouse. The $600,000 will be subject to estate tax; the estate tax on the $600,000 is $192,800. The estate tax *credit* on the transfer is also $192,800. Therefore, the estate tax due from the taxable transfer of the $600,000 is zero. That is, the tax is exactly offset by the credit.

However, using the unlimited marital deduction, if you leave all of your assets to your spouse, you will lose the first death credit since nothing was subject to tax. This will result in a $600,000 increase in the spouse's estate. Although the spouse also gets a credit of $192,800 (against the $600,000 in assets), since you didn't use the credit on the first death, the estate pays more in taxes on the second death. If the asset worth $600,000 was taxed on the first death, all appreciation on that asset passes tax free at the second death. If it wasn't taxed, you lose the credit, and the appreciation is also taxed in the spouse's estate.

Let's assume you have a $5 million estate. You can use the unlimited marital deduction and transfer all of the estate to your spouse; at her death, assuming that the $5 million is intact, her estate would have a tax liability of $2.198 million. However, if on your death you pass $600,000 to a "bypass" trust and allow it to be subject to tax, $192,800 in tax is off-set by the credit. The amount due is still zero on the first death. The use of the bypass trust would save the estate on the second death the $192,000, as well as taxes due on any appreciation of that asset.

8. **Having a bank act as sole trustee of your marital trust with no provision for the income beneficiary (your wife) to change trustees.** Your local banker probably has known you for years as a local businessman and for your community involvement. However, you cannot expect that the services provided to you will also be provided to your spouse. Your banker may not even know her.

It is important, therefore, to afford your spouse the right to change the corporate trustee. Giving your spouse the right to change the trustee, a limited power in the trust document, keeps the bank "on its toes" and more attentive to providing services to your spouse.

However, it is important that your spouse cannot appoint herself as the successor trustee, since that would result in those assets being included in the spouse's estate for tax purposes. By *not* having the right to change the corporate trustee, your spouse is locked into the bank as trustee, regardless of the bank's services, how the assets are managed, and the income the bank derives on the investments. Your spouse would have no ability to move the funds from that bank to any other bank or any other institution within or outside the state.

If your spouse should move out of state, she would always be subject to the trust department of the local bank managing her assets, even though she may live many miles away. Giving her the ability to change to another corporate trustee provides flexibility for your spouse and an additional measure of security.

9. **Improper titling of assets.** Often assets are improperly titled. You may not realize that the manner in which the asset is titled may take precedence over your will in describing how that asset is transferred in the estate. For example, although your will may say that your assets go in trust for your spouse, if in fact they are titled as joint tenants with rights of survivorship, your assets will pass directly to her and bypass any trust arrangements you have created. Sometimes life insurance trusts are established but the beneficiary designations are never changed on the policy. One client was surprised to find that an old life insurance policy still named his first wife as beneficiary, even though they had been divorced for ten years. When coordinating the transfer of business inter-ests, it is important to check the stock certificates since they are often issued differently than everyone remembers.

In one example, a business owner assumed that business real estate was titled in the corporate name. However, in checking records, he determined that when he had incorporated his business 10 years earlier, the real estate had never been transferred into the corporation. Although from a planning standpoint, we were happy to learn that the real estate was outside the company, the accountant was extremely upset since he had been treating the real estate as a corporate asset and depreciating it on the corporate books. Furthermore, the company had never paid rent to the owner since everyone thought the real estate was in the corporation.

With proper planning, a substantial amount of estate tax liabilities can be either eliminated or significantly reduced. Rather than retaining assets in the estate that increase in value, it may be better to enter into contractual arrangements through a stock purchase agreement with your corporation or create transfer plans with family members to provide for the transfer of ownership.

It is also important to create liquidity. Liquid or income producing assets can provide income to other family members. Sell business assets during your lifetime to other family members or key employees. Keep business interests out of the estate. Enter into ownership arrangements with other family members to reduce the value of the estate for estate tax purposes. Plan now to provide income for your spouse and children, and business opportunities for new entrepreneurs in your family. Reduce taxation in the estate that will occur on either the first or second death.

Lifetime business planning can be the most important estate planning you ever do.

27

Epilogue

IN THIS BOOK WE'VE EXPLORED A NUMBER OF "HOW-TO'S": HOW TO TRANSFER A family business, how to maintain and preserve family wealth, how to recognize the obstacles to a transfer.

Values and ideas must be consciously shared. Your children or successors cannot share your goals through osmosis. You need to talk with them. Share with them. Explain to them why you do the things you do and make the decisions you make.

This communication should begin with children at an early age. The family business is a unique environment for children as they grow up. Children can learn to feel part of that business environment and to love the business.

The family business is constantly changing. It is not static. It evolves over time just as its individual members evolve. The evolution of the family business can benefit those who are part of it and stay with it. Continued personal growth that leads to greater fulfillment, family growth that leads to greater harmony, and business growth that leads to economic success are the by-products of passing the torch. Those who see this as an adventure, a challenging opportunity, and a potentially rewarding experience have the greatest chance of succeeding with their business transfer.

Your future, and the future of your children, will be built on the plans you design and implement today. Your successor's ideas and dreams should be part of those plans. Respect and communication between you and your successors will give you both the incentive to make the transfer a success. Family business and business families can help each other mature.

There can be a dynamic balance between the present and the future, the aging owner and the younger successor.

The plans you put in place today will impact you, your family, and your business for years to come. If you haven't already started, you should begin now.

Appendix A
Calculating Your Need for Retirement Income

The present worth of $1 is a $1. At 10%, however, $1 will grow to $1.10 in one year. The future worth of a dollar in one year is, thus, $1.10, and in two years it is $1.21.

Future Worth of a Present Dollar—Table A-1

Table A-1 is useful in evaluating what a lump sum today will accumulate to in the future, assuming compounding at different interest rates.

Table A-1. Future Worth of Present Dollar $(1 + i)^N$

Years Hence	1%	3%	5%	6%	7%	8%	9%	10%
1	1.010	1.030	1.050	1.060	1.070	1.080	1.090	1.100
2	1.020	1.061	1.102	1.124	1.145	1.166	1.186	1.210
3	1.030	1.093	1.158	1.191	1.225	1.260	1.295	1.331
4	1.041	1.126	1.216	1.262	1.311	1.360	1.412	1.464
5	1.051	1.159	1.276	1.338	1.403	1.469	1.539	1.611
6	1.062	1.194	1.340	1.419	1.501	1.587	1.677	1.772
7	1.072	1.230	1.407	1.504	1.606	1.714	1.828	1.949
8	1.083	1.267	1.477	1.594	1.718	1.851	1.993	2.144
9	1.094	1.305	1.551	1.689	1.838	1.999	2.172	2.358
10	1.105	1.344	1.629	1.791	1.967	2.159	2.367	2.594
11	1.116	1.384	1.710	1.898	2.105	2.332	2.580	2.853
12	1.127	1.426	1.796	2.012	2.252	2.518	2.813	3.138
13	1.138	1.469	1.886	2.133	2.410	2.720	3.066	3.452
14	1.149	1.513	1.980	2.261	2.579	2.937	3.342	3.797
15	1.161	1.558	2.079	2.397	2.759	3.172	3.642	4.177
20	1.220	1.806	2.653	3.207	3.870	4.661	5.604	6.728
25	1.282	2.094	3.386	4.292	5.427	6.848	8.623	10.835
30	1.348	2.427	4.322	5.743	7.612	10.063	13.268	17.449

Table value for the specified   Initial   Total
time period and interest rate × Amount = Accumulated

         2.759   × $10,000 = $27,590
     (7%, 15 Years)

Continued

_____Table A-1. Continued._____

Years Hence	12%	14%	15%	16%	18%	20%	24%	36%
1	1.120	1.140	1.150	1.160	1.180	1.200	1.240	1.360
2	1.254	1.300	1.322	1.346	1.392	1.440	1.538	1.850
3	1.405	1.482	1.521	1.561	1.643	1.728	1.907	2.515
4	1.574	1.689	1.749	1.811	1.939	2.074	2.364	3.421
5	1.762	1.925	2.011	2.100	2.288	2.488	2.932	4.653
6	1.974	2.195	2.313	2.436	2.700	2.986	3.635	6.328
7	2.211	2.502	2.660	2.826	3.185	3.583	4.508	8.605
8	2.476	2.853	3.059	3.278	3.759	4.300	5.590	11.703
9	2.773	3.252	3.518	3.803	4.435	5.160	6.931	15.917
10	3.106	3.707	4.046	4.411	5.234	6.192	8.594	21.647
11	3.479	4.226	4.652	5.117	6.176	7.430	10.657	29.439
12	3.896	4.818	5.350	5.926	7.288	8.916	13.215	40.037
13	4.363	5.492	6.153	6.886	8.599	10.699	16.386	54.451
14	4.887	6.261	7.076	7.988	10.147	12.839	20.319	74.053
15	5.474	7.138	8.137	9.266	11.974	15.407	25.196	100.712
20	9.646	13.743	16.367	19.461	27.393	38.338	73.864	468.570
25	17.000	26.462	32.919	40.874	62.669	95.396	216.542	2180.100
30	29.960	50.950	66.212	85.850	143.371	237.376	634.820	10143.000

7.138   × $10,000 = $71,380
(14%, 15 Years)

_____Financial Independence/Retirement_____

Income desired per month, current dollars:	$ 6,000
Estimated social security, current dollars:	− 1,125
	$ 4,875

SCENARIO

	A	B
Number of years to retirement (from age 50):	15	15
Assumed inflation rate during the period:	3%	5%
Net need at assumed inflation rate		
A. 3% in 15 years:	7,595/month (Table A-1: 4,875 × 1,558)	
B. 5% in 15 years:		10,135/month (Table A-1: 4,875 × 2,079)
Annual requirement:	$91,140	$121,620

Continued

Less projected income from existing
retirement plans and other investments:

Present investments:	$200,000
Future worth factor:	4.177 (Table A-1)
(If invested at 10% for 15 years)	
Future worth in 15 years:	$835,400

This amount is anticipated to earn 10% before taxes
over a 20-year period, will provide an annual income of: $98,121 $98,121
 ($835,400 divided by 8.514 (Table A-4))

Annual income still required at retirement: $ – $23,499

Additional assets needed at age 65 to provide monthly
income for a 20-year period, assuming 10% before tax return: $ – $200,070
 ($23,499 times 8.514 (Table A-4))

Investments required to provide assets needed at age 65:	Annual Investment Required	
Assuming a 6% annual rate of return	$ 8,596	($200,070 divided by 23.276 (Table A-3))
Assuming a 8% annual rate of return	$ 7,369	($200,070 divided by 27.152 (Table A-3))
Assuming a 10% annual rate of return	$ 6,297	($200,070 divided by 31.772 (Table A-3))
Assuming a 14% annual rate of return	$ 4,563	($200,070 divided by 43.842 (Table A-3))

Future Worth of a Present Dollar

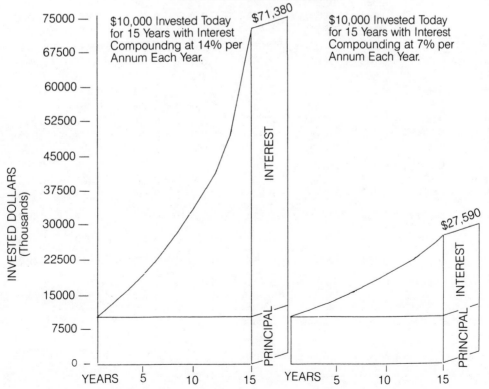

Present Worth of a Future Dollar—Table A-2

The opposite of what a present dollar will accumulate to in the future is the present worth of a future dollar. Mathematically, the present worth of a future dollar is less than a dollar by whatever the going interest rate is, and measured by whatever period of time will elapse before the dollar is received. This process is called discounting, and the value of a future dollar today is called its present value.

If you had a desire to accumulate a fund to $10,000 at the end of five years and you were guaranteed a return of 15% compounded annually, how much would you have to deposit today? $4,970.

This table is also useful in dealing with inflation. For example, if you are to receive $1 one year from now, and the present annual rate of inflation is 10%, that dollar is worth only $.909 today.

Table A-2. Present Value of a Future Dollar $(1 + i)^{-N}$

Years Hence	1%	6%	8%	10%	12%	14%	15%	16%
1	0.990	0.943	0.926	0.909	0.893	0.877	0.870	0.862
2	0.980	0.890	0.857	0.826	0.797	0.769	0.756	0.743
3	0.971	0.840	0.794	0.751	0.712	0.675	0.658	0.641
4	0.961	0.792	0.735	0.683	0.636	0.592	0.572	0.552
5	0.951	0.747	0.681	0.621	0.567	0.519	0.497	0.476
6	0.942	0.705	0.630	0.564	0.507	0.456	0.432	0.410
7	0.933	0.665	0.583	0.513	0.452	0.400	0.376	0.354
8	0.923	0.627	0.540	0.467	0.404	0.351	0.327	0.305
9	0.914	0.592	0.500	0.424	0.361	0.308	0.284	0.263
10	0.905	0.558	0.463	0.386	0.322	0.270	0.247	0.227
11	0.896	0.527	0.429	0.350	0.287	0.237	0.215	0.195
12	0.887	0.497	0.397	0.319	0.257	0.208	0.187	0.168
13	0.879	0.469	0.368	0.290	0.229	0.182	0.163	0.145
14	0.870	0.442	0.340	0.263	0.205	0.160	0.141	0.125
15	0.861	0.417	0.315	0.239	0.183	0.140	0.123	0.108
20	0.820	0.312	0.215	0.149	0.104	0.073	0.061	0.051
25	0.780	0.233	0.146	0.092	0.059	0.038	0.030	0.024
30	0.742	0.174	0.099	0.057	0.033	0.020	0.015	0.012
40	0.672	0.097	0.046	0.022	0.011	0.005	0.004	0.003

Table value for the specified   Future   Present
time period and interest rate × Amount = Value

.497
(15%, 5 Years) × $10,000 = $4,970

Personal Cash Flow Projection
for Mom and Dad
(Years 1 through 5)

	Year 1	Year 2	Year 3	Year 4	Year 5
Dad's age	57	58	59	60	61
Mom's age	55	56	57	58	59
Sources of funds:					
Salaries	$100,000	$0			
Consulting Agreements	37,500	75,000	75,000	75,000	75,000
Supplemental Pensions					
Noncompete Agreements	23,000	46,000	46,000	46,000	46,000
Stock Redemption Note	79,290	158,581	158,581	158,581	158,581
Net Rental Income —					
Real Estate	3,000	3,000	3,000	3,000	3,000
Sale of Real Estate					
Other Income	1,500	1,500	1,500	1,500	1,500
Dividends & Interest	5,000	5,000	5,000	5,000	5,000
Social Security and Profit Sharing					
Life Insurance Proceeds					
Investment Income on Excess Cash Flow, if Invested in Tax-frees at 6%	0	3,172	7,220	12,084	16,814
TOTAL SOURCES	249,290	292,253	296,301	301,165	305,895
Uses of funds:					
Cost of Lifestyle	100,000	104,000	108,160	112,486	116,986
College Tuition for 2 Kids	15,000	32,400	17,500	18,900	20,400
Home Mortgage	24,000	24,000	24,000	24,000	24,000
Vacations	8,000	8,320	8,653	8,999	9,359
Income and FICA Taxes	49,424	56,061	56,928	57,942	58,937
TOTAL NEED	196,424	224,781	215,241	222,327	229,682
Annual Margin <Deficit>	$52,867	$67,472	$81,060	$78,837	$76,213
Cumulative Cash Flow <Deficit>	$52,867	$120,339	$201,399	$280,236	$356,450

	Personal Cash Flow Projection for Mom and Dad (Years 6 through 10)				
	Year 6	Year 7	Year 8	Year 9	Year 10
Dad's age	62	63	64	65	66
Mom's age	60	61	62	63	64
Sources of funds:					
Salaries					
Consulting Agreements	37,500	0			
Supplemental Pensions	41,500	83,000	83,000	83,000	83,000
Noncompete Agreements	23,000	0			
Stock Redemption Note	158,581	158,581	158,581	158,581	158,581
Net Rental Income —-					
Real Estate	3,000	3,000	3,000	3,000	1,500
Sale of Real Estate					43,426
Other Income	1,500	1,500	1,500	1,500	1,500
Dividends & Interest	5,000	5,000	5,000	5,000	5,000
Social Security and Profit Sharing				30,937	31,299
Life Insurance Proceeds					
Investment Income on Excess Cash Flow, if Invested in Tax-frees at 6%	21,387	26,360	30,496	35,709	42,616
TOTAL SOURCES	291,468	277,441	281,577	317,727	366,922
Uses of funds:					
Cost of Lifestyle	121,665	126,532	131,593	136,857	142,331
College Tuition for 2 Kids	0				
Home Mortgage	24,000	24,000	4,000	0	
Vacations	9,733	10,123	10,527	10,949	11,386
Income and FICA Taxes	53,179	47,858	48,572	54,808	63,294
TOTAL NEED	208,578	208,512	194,693	202,613	217,012
Annual Margin <Deficit>	$82,890	$68,929	$86,884	$115,114	$149,910
Cumulative Cash Flow <Deficit>	$439,340	$508,269	$595,153	$710,267	$860,177

------------------------------------Personal Cash Flow Projection------------------------------------
for Mom and Dad
(Years 15 through 30)

	Year 15	Year 20	Year 24	Year 25	Year 30
Dad's age	71	76	80		
Mom's age	69	74	78	79	84
Sources of funds:					
Salaries					
Consulting Agreements					
Supplemental Pensions	83,000	83,000			
Noncompete Agreements					
Stock Redemption Note					
Net Rental Income —					
Real Estate					
Sale of Real Estate	86,852	86,852	86,582	86,852	43,426
Other Income	1,500	1,500	1,500	1,500	1,500
Dividends & Interest	5,000	5,000	5,000	5,000	5,000
Social Security and					
Profit Sharing	56,601	61,056	65,127	47,424	50,418
Life Insurance Proceeds			500,000		
Investment Income on					
Excess Cash Flow,					
if Invested in Tax-frees at 6%	72,831	90,249	87,631	113,879	85,019
TOTAL SOURCES	305,784	327,657	746,109	254,654	185,363
Uses of funds:					
Cost of Lifestyle	173,168	210,685	246,472	256,330	311,865
College Tuition for 2 Kids					
Home Mortgage					
Vacations	13,853	16,855	19,718	20,506	24,949
Income and FICA Taxes	52,748	56,521	42,453	43,928	31,975
TOTAL NEED	239,769	284,061	308,642	320,765	368,789
Annual Margin <Deficit>	$66,015	$43,596	$437,467	($66,110)	($183,427)
Cumulative Cash					
Flow <Deficit>	$1,279,871	$1,547,744	$1,897,976	$1,831,865	$1,223,553

PERSONAL CASH FLOW PROJECTION—NOTES AND ASSUMPTIONS

1. *Salaries.* Salaries for both Dad and Mom are assumed to stop at the end of June, Year 1.

2. *Consulting Agreements, Supplemental Pensions, Noncompete Covenants, and Redemption Note.* Payments under these agreements are projected as described in the overview.

3. *Rental Income—Real Estate*. Net rental income is projected as follows:

Rents	$58,800
Mortgage payments	(44,000)
Insurance	(2,500)
Taxes	(9,000)
Accounting fees	(300)
	$3,000

Rents received, as well as expenses other than the mortgage, are projected to increase by 5% per year. Client expects to accelerate the mortgage payments in future years in order to retire the mortgage in Year 10.

4. *Sale of Real Estate*. It is assumed that the real estate which houses the Company's offices is sold to the three active children after the expiration of the existing lease and renewals, in Year 10. The value at that time is projected to be $750,000, which is paid by a note at 10% over 20 years.

5. *Other Income*. Other income is projected based on the actual average for the past three years. The income is assumed to remain level throughout both Dad and Mom's lifetimes.

6. *Dividends & Interest*. The income is projected for Year 1 based on the prior year's amount. Additional investment income is projected separately.

7. *Social Security*. Benefits are projected to begin at age 65 for both Dad and Mom, and are estimated using the Year 1 benefit schedule increased by 3% annually.

8. *Profit-Sharing Plan*. The existing balances in the profit sharing plan accounts are assumed to earn 8% annually. Distributions are assumed to begin at age 65 and are based on a 6% joint and 100% survivor annuity.

9. *Life Insurance Proceeds*. Proceeds of personally-owned life insurance are assumed to be payable to Mom at Dad's death. Dad is assumed to live to age 80, and Mom is assumed to live to age 85.

10. *Investment Income*. The investment income projected assumes that excess cumulative cash flow is invested in tax-free investments yielding 6%.

11. *Cost of Lifestyle*. The current cost of lifestyle, excluding items listed separately, is estimated by the client to be $88,000, and is assumed to grow at 4% per year.

12. *College Tuition*. College tuition is projected for one child through Year 2 and for another child beginning in Year 2 through Year 5, based on current rates with 8% per year increases.

13. *Home Mortgage*. The home mortgage is projected to continue at $2,000 per month through maturity in February, Year 8.

14. *Vacation.* Vacation costs are estimated by the client and assumed to grow at 4% per year.

15. *Taxes.* FICA taxes are projected using the current FICA tax rate. Salaries and consulting agreements are assumed to be subject to FICA taxes. Federal income taxes are projected at 15% of total funds sources, excluding life insurance proceeds. State income taxes are projected at 15% of the Federal tax.

Notes

Chapter 3. Establishing Clear Goals

1. John Ward, *Keeping the Family Business Healthy* (San Francisco: Jossey-Bass, 1987), 16.

Chapter 4. Solving Family Conflicts

1. Rosenblatt, et. al., *The Family in Business* (San Francisco: Jossey-Bass, 1985), 21.
2. Ibid.
3. Ivan Lansberg, "The Succession Conspiracy," *Family Business Review*, vol. 1, no. 2, (1988): 123.
4. Rosenblatt, 16.
5. John Ward, *Keeping the Family Business Healthy* (San Francisco: Jossey-Bass, 1987), 54.
6. Robert Fisher and William Ury, *Getting to Yes: Negotiating Agreement Without Giving In* (Penguin Books, 1983).
7. Ervin Laszlo, *The Systems View of the World* (New York: George Braziller, Inc., 1972), 75.

Chapter 5. Recognizing the Stages of Life

1. Daniel J. Levinson, *The Seasons of a Man's Life* (New York: Ballantine Books, 1978), 18.

Chapter 6. Establishing the Family Commitment

1. Edwin Crego, Jr., Brian Deaton, and Peter Schiffrin, "How to Write a Business Plan" (American Management Association, Extension Institute, 2nd edition, 1986).

Chapter 11. What's Your Business Worth?

1. Orville B. Lefko, "Buy/Sell Agreements and Appraisals," *Michigan State Bar Journal*, (February 1976): 116.

Chapter 12. Valuation Discounts: Manipulating the Value of Your Business

1. Ray Consolidated Copper Company vs. United States, 45 S. Ct. 526 (1925).
2. Shannon Pratt, *Valuing a Business*, 2nd Edition (Dow Jones-Erwin, 1989), 239.
3. Ibid., 389.
4. Ibid., 368.
5. *Estate Planning*, Spring, 1975, 141, and *Estate Planning*, September, 1983, 282.
6. J. Michael Maher, "Discounts for Lack of Marketability for Closely Held Business Interests," *Taxes*, (September, 1976): 562-571.
7. Revenue Ruling 77-287, (1977-2 C.B. 319), Sect. 1.
8. Securities & Exchange Commission, Acct. Series Release #113: Statement regarding restricted securities (Chicago: Commerce Clearing House, Federal Securities Law Reports, 1977), 62, 285.
9. J. Michael Maher, "An Objective Measure for a Discount for a Minority Interest and a Premium for a Controlling Interest," *Taxes*, (July, 1979): 451.

Chapter 15. Transfer Strategy # 2: Transfer of Stocks

1. IRC Sec. 2036 (c).

Chapter 16. Transfer Strategy # 3: Offset Sales

1. U.S. Court of Claims, Ullman vs. Commissioner, (Second CIR, 1959).
2. Schulz vs. Commissioner, (9th Circuit, 1961).
3. See Freeport Transportation, Inc., 63%C 107 (1974).

Chapter 24. Creative Property Ownership Interests

1. *Readings in Estate Planning*, ed. by Ted Kurlowicz (The American College, 1987), 2.1.

Bibliography

Cooper, George. *A Voluntary Tax? New Perspectives on Sophisticated Estate Tax Avoidance,* Washington, DC: The Brookings Institution, 1979.

Danco, L.A. *Beyond Survival: A Business Owner's Guide for Success,* Cleveland, OH: University Press, 1982.

_____. *Inside the Family Business,* Cleveland, OH: University Press, 1980.

Dyer, W. Gibb, Jr. *Cultural Change in Family Firms,* San Francisco: Jossey-Bass, 1986.

Edinberg, Mark A. *Talking with Your Aging Parents,* Boston: Shambhala Publications, 1987.

Eliot, Dr. Robert S. and Breo, Dennis L., *Is it Worth Dying for?,* New York: Bantam Books, 1984.

Erikson, Erik H. *Childhood and Society,* New York: W. W. Norton & Co., 1963.

Fisher, Robert and Ury, William. *Getting to Yes, Negotiating Agreement without Giving in,* New York: Penguin Books, 1983.

Flamholtz, Eric G. *How to Make the Transition from an Entrepreneurship to a Professionally Managed Firm,* San Francisco: Jossey-Bass, 1986.

Laing, R.D. *The Politics of the Family and Other Essays,* New York: Vintage Books, 1971.

Laszlo, Ervin. *The Systems View of the World,* New York: George Braziller, Inc., 1972.

Leimberg, Stephan R., et. al. *Financial Services Professionals Guide to the State of the Art/1989,* Bryn Mawr, PA: The American College, 1989.

Levinson, D.J. *The Seasons of A Man's Life,* New York: Ballantine Books, 1978.

McQuaig, Jack H. *Your Business Your Son and You,* Coral Springs, FL: B. Klein Publications, 1979.

Maslow, A.H. *Eupsychian Management,* Homewood, IL: Richard D. Irwin, Inc., 1965.

_____. *The Farther Reaches of Human Nature,* New York: The Viking Press, 1971.

_____. *Toward A Psychology of Being,* New York; Van Nostrand Reinhold Co., 1968.

Myers, Albert and Andersen, Christopher P. *Success Over Sixty,* New York: Summit Books, 1984.

Peters, Tom. *Thriving on Chais,* New York: Alfred A. Knopf, 1988.

Peters, T.J. and Waterman, R.H., Jr. *In Search of Excellence,* New York: Harper & Row, 1982.

Pratt, Shannon P. *Valuing A Business,* Homewood, IL: Dow Jones-Irwin, Second Edition, 1989.

Rosenblatt, P.C., de Mik, L., Anderson, R.M., and Johnson, P.A. *The Family in Business,* San Francisco: Jossey-Bass, 1985.

Russell, G. Hugh, and Black, Kenneth, Jr. *Human Behavior in Business,* Englewood Cliffs, NJ: Prentice-Hall, 1972.

Scarf, Maggie. *Intimate Partners,* New York: Ballantine Books, 1987.

Sheehy, Gail. *Passages: Predictable Crises of Adult Life,* New York: Bantam Books, 1977.

Ward, John. *Keeping the Family Business Healthy,* San Francisco: Jossey-Bass, 1987.

Waterman, Robert H., Jr. *The Renewal Factor,* New York: Bantam Books, 1987.

Index

Future Worth of an Annuity—Table A-3

If you added $1 per year for 20 years and it was earning 10%, it would have grown to $57.275; $20 would represent the $1 annual contribution and $37.275 would have been interest.

Table A-3 is useful in calculating what will accumulate under a systematic savings or investment plan.

Table A-3. Future Worth of an Annuity $\dfrac{(1 + i)^{N-1}}{i}$

Years Hence	1%	3%	5%	6%	7%	8%	9%	10%
1	1.000	1.000	1.000	1.000	1.000	1.000	1.000	1.000
2	2.010	2.030	2.050	2.060	2.070	2.080	2.090	2.100
3	3.030	3.091	3.152	3.184	3.215	3.246	3.278	3.310
4	4.060	4.184	4.310	4.375	4.440	4.506	4.573	4.641
5	5.101	5.309	5.526	5.637	5.751	5.867	5.985	6.105
6	6.152	6.468	6.802	6.975	7.153	7.336	7.523	7.716
7	7.214	7.662	8.142	8.394	8.654	8.923	9.200	9.487
8	8.286	8.892	9.549	9.897	10.260	10.637	11.028	11.436
9	9.369	10.159	11.027	11.491	11.978	12.488	13.021	13.579
10	10.462	11.464	12.578	13.181	13.816	14.487	15.193	15.937
11	11.567	12.808	14.207	14.972	15.784	16.645	17.560	18.531
12	12.683	14.192	15.917	16.870	17.888	18.977	20.141	21.384
13	13.809	15.618	17.713	18.882	20.141	21.495	22.953	24.523
14	14.947	17.086	19.599	21.051	22.550	24.215	26.019	27.975
15	16.097	18.599	21.579	23.276	25.129	27.152	29.361	31.772
20	22.019	26.870	33.066	36.786	40.995	45.762	51.160	57.275
25	28.243	36.459	47.727	54.865	63.249	73.106	84.701	98.347
30	34.785	47.575	66.439	79.058	94.461	113.283	136.308	164.494

Table value for the specified   Annuity   Total
time period and interest rate × Amount = Accumulated

    57.275
    (10%, 20 Years) × $1   = $57.28

Years Hence	12%	14%	16%	18%	20%	24%	36%
1	1.000	1.000	1.000	1.000	1.000	1.000	1.000
2	2.120	2.140	2.160	2.180	2.200	2.240	2.360
3	3.374	3.440	3.506	3.572	3.640	3.778	4.210
4	4.770	4.921	5.066	5.215	5.368	5.684	6.725
5	6.353	6.610	6.877	7.154	7.442	8.048	10.146

Table A-3. Continued. Future Worth of an Annuity $\dfrac{(1 + i)^{N-1}}{i}$

6	8.115	8.536	8.977	9.442	9.930	10.980	14.799
7	10.089	10.730	11.414	12.142	12.916	14.615	21.126
8	12.300	13.233	14.240	15.327	16.499	19.123	29.732
9	14.776	16.085	17.518	19.086	20.799	24.712	41.435
10	17.549	19.337	21.321	23.521	25.959	31.643	57.352
11	20.655	23.044	25.733	28.755	32.150	40.238	78.998
12	24.133	27.271	30.850	34.931	39.580	50.985	105.437
13	28.029	32.089	36.786	42.219	48.497	64.110	148.475
14	32.393	37.581	43.672	50.818	59.196	80.495	202.926
15	37.280	43.842	51.660	60.965	72.035	100.815	276.979
20	72.052	91.025	115.380	146.628	186.688	303.601	1298.800
25	133.334	181.871	249.214	342.603	471.981	898.092	6053.000
30	241.333	356.787	530.312	790.948	1181.882	2640.916	28172.000

43.842   × $1,000 = $43,842
(14%, 15 Years)

Future Worth of an Annuity

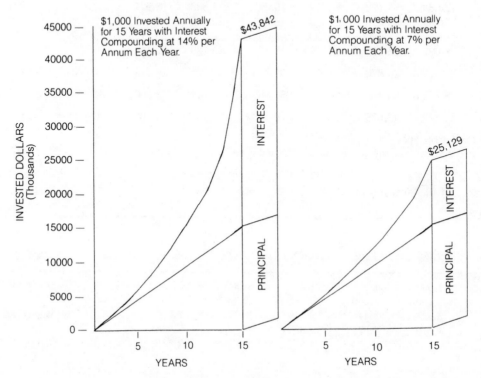

$1,000 Invested Annually for 15 Years with Interest Compounding at 14% per Annum Each Year.

$1,000 Invested Annually for 15 Years with Interest Compounding at 7% per Annum Each Year.

$43,842

$25,129

INVESTED DOLLARS (Thousands)

INTEREST

PRINCIPAL

YEARS

Present Worth of a Future Annuity—Table A-4

The final formula relates to the Present Worth of a Future Annuity.

Table A-4 represents the lump sum today which has the same value as a string of periodic future payments based upon a certain period of time and a specified interest rate. As an example, at 10% compounded annually, $8,514 today is equal to 20 annual payments of $1,000 each. This formula is useful in retirement planning.

Table A-4. Present Worth of a Future Dollar Received $\frac{(1 + i)^{N-1}}{i}$ Annually for N Years.

Years Hence	1%	6%	8%	10%	12%	14%	15%	16%
1	0.990	0.943	0.926	0.909	0.893	0.877	0.870	0.862
2	1.970	1.833	1.783	1.736	1.690	1.647	1.626	1.605
3	2.941	2.673	2.577	2.487	2.402	2.322	2.283	2.246
4	3.902	3.465	3.312	3.170	3.037	2.914	2.855	2.798
5	4.853	4.212	3.993	3.791	3.605	3.433	3.352	3.274
6	5.795	4.917	4.623	4.355	4.111	3.889	3.784	3.685
7	6.728	5.582	5.206	4.868	4.564	4.288	4.160	4.039
8	7.652	6.210	5.747	5.335	4.968	4.639	4.487	4.344
9	8.566	6.802	6.247	5.759	5.328	4.946	4.772	4.607
10	9.471	7.360	6.710	6.145	5.650	5.216	5.019	4.833
11	10.368	7.887	7.139	6.495	5.988	5.453	5.234	5.029
12	11.255	8.384	7.536	6.814	6.194	5.660	5.421	5.197
13	12.134	8.853	7.904	7.103	6.424	5.842	5.583	5.342
14	13.004	9.295	8.244	7.367	6.628	6.002	5.724	5.468
15	13.865	9.712	8.559	7.606	6.811	6.142	5.847	5.575
20	18.046	11.47	9.818	8.514	7.469	6.623	6.259	5.929
25	22.023	12.783	10.675	9.077	7.843	6.873	6.464	6.097
30	25.808	13.765	11.258	9.427	8.055	7.003	6.566	6.177
40	32.835	15.046	11.925	9.779	8.244	7.105	6.642	6.234

Table value for the specified time period and interest rate × Annuity Amount = Total Present Value

8.514 × $5,149.60 = $43,842
(10%, 20 Years)

Appendix B
Sample Buy-Out by Children

Dad and Mom own 90 percent of Dad's Manufacturing Company. Dad estimates that if the company were to be sold to a publicly-held corporation, its value would be calculated at about $3,000,000. The book value of Dad's Manufacturing Company is $560,000.

In the past, Dad and Mom have made gifts of stock in the company to three of their children who are active in the business, Son No. 1, Son No. 2, and Daughter. The gifted stock totals 10 percent of the ownership of the company.

The parents now wish to transfer the balance of the company ownership in such a way that the three active children own the entire company, one-third each. Currently, Dad owns 4,800 shares, Mom owns 600 shares, and each active child owns 200 shares.

The following pages outline how the transaction may be structured to provide Dad and Mom $2.7 million through a combination of agreements between the current owners and the manufacturing company. The cash-flow projection illustrates the impact this will have on the company and its cash flow.

Following the corporate cash flow is a personal cash-flow outline for Dad and Mom. They wanted to be assured that the transfer of the business interests would not conflict with their personal need for financial security. By detailing both the sources and uses, and the timing sequences, Dad and Mom felt that the "annual margin" they would have would provide the financial cushion they want.

Table B-1. Business Ownership Dad's Manufacturing Company

Stockholder	No. of Shares	% of Shares	Book	Values at Year-End Adjusted Book	Industry Standard	Cap. Earn. Method
Dad	4,800	80.0%	$448,000	$712,000	$2,400,000	$800,000
Mom	600	10.0%	$56,000	$89,000	$300,000	$100,000
Son #1	200	3.3%	$18,667	$29,667	$100,000	$33,333
Son #2	200	3.3%	$18,667	$29,667	$100,000	$33,333
Daughter	200	3.3%	$18,667	$29,667	$100,000	$33,333
Totals	6,000	100.0%	$560,000	$890,000	$3,000,000	$1,000,000
Per Share Value			$93	$148	$500	$167

Dad's Manufacturing Company
Determination of Redemption Price
(SALE ASSUMED ON JULY 1)

Redemption price should be:

- not less than book value.
- not less than a reasonable fair market value, to avoid any potential assertion of a gift to the children, who are stockholders.

All values have been discounted 20% for lack of marketability.

Value of Dad
and Mom's 90%

$2,160,000	*Value No. 1:*	Industry standard; one times the average of three years' gross revenues.
$720,000	*Value No. 2:*	Capitalized earnings method; calculated based on historical earnings in excess of a normal return on the operating assets.
$403,200	*Value No. 3:*	Book value; the excess of the company's assets over its liabilities.

Based on this analysis, a redemption price of $1,000,000 for Dad and Mom's stock appears reasonable.

Dad's Manufacturing Company

Redemption Offer to Dad and Mom

	Total Cash	Present Value
Stock Redemption note, 10%, payable $13,215.07 monthly for 10 years	$1,000,000	$1,000,000

Agreements and Retirement Benefits for Dad and Mom

Consulting agreements:

	Total Cash	Present Value
Dad: $50,000 per year for 3 years, paid monthly	$150,000	$129,130
Mom: $25,000 per year for 3 years, paid monthly	75,000	64,565
	$225,000	$193,695

Continued

_____Dad's Manufacturing Company. Continued._____

Noncompete covenants:

Dad: $30,000 per year for 5 years, paid monthly	$150,000	$117,663
Mom: $16,000 per year for 5 years, paid monthly	80,000	62,754
	$230,000	$180,417

Supplemental pensions:

Dad: $4,667 per month for 15 years, beginning at age 62	$840,000	$269,666
Mom: $2,250 per month for 15 years, beginning at age 60	405,000	130,008
	$1,245,000	$399,674
Total	$2,700,000	$1,773,786

REDEMPTION AND RETIREMENT PLANNING—AN OVERVIEW

The projection assumes that the corporation redeems Dad's and Mom's stock in Dad's Manufacturing Company. They continue to lease to the company the real estate where the offices are located, on a three-year lease with the company having the option to renew the lease for 2 three-year terms. In the 10th year of the projection, we have assumed that the children have exercised an option to purchase the real estate from their parents for its fair market value at that time.

These payments are reflected in the cash-flow projections for the company and for Dad and Mom:

- Note payments to Dad: $1,000,000 payable $13,215.07 monthly including interest at 10%, for ten years, beginning July 1, Year 1.
- Consulting agreements: payments to Dad of $4,167 and Mom of $2,083 monthly from July, Year 1 through June, Year 4.
- Noncompete covenants: payments to Dad of $2,500 and Mom of $1,333 monthly from July, Year 1 through June, Year 6.
- Supplemental pensions: monthly payments of $4,667 to Dad and $2,250 to Mom beginning in July, Year 6, for 15 years.
- Rents: $4,900 monthly to Dad and Mom for the real estate, beginning July, Year 1, with 5% per year increases through June, Year 10.

_____**Dad's Manufacturing Company**_____
Cash Flow Projection
(For the year ending December 31)

Projected future years

	Year 1	*Year 2*	*Year 3*	*Year 5*	*Year 10*
Sales Trend		−4%	+12.5%	−4%	+5%
Sales—Net	$3,113,000	$2,988,480	$3,362,040	$3,388,936	$4,539,607
Cost of Sales	2,116,840	2,032,166	2,286,187	2,304,477	3,086,933
Gross Profit	996,160	956,314	1,075,853	1,084,460	1,452,674
Operating Expenses					
Owners' Salaries					
Dad	75,000	0	0	0	0
Mom	25,000	0	0	0	0
Son #1	42,500	52,000	54,080	58,493	71,166
Son #2	20,000	20,800	25,000	31,200	37,960
Daughter	17,200	17,888	22,000	26,000	31,633
Bonuses					
Consulting Agreements	37,500	75,000	75,000	75,000	0
Supplemental Pensions	0	0	0	0	83,000
Other Salaries	251,320	261,373	271,828	294,009	357,707
Profit Sharing Plan	21,551	17,603	18,645	20,485	24,923
Rents—Offices	58,800	61,740	64,827	71,472	91,218
Other Expenses	284,544	269,530	274,509	283,584	306,266
Noncompete Convenants	23,000	46,000	46,000	46,000	0
Total Operating Expenses	856,415	826,762	861,737	926,743	1,054,962
Income from Operations	139,745	129,552	214,116	157,717	397,712
Miscellaneous Income	13,000	13,520	14,061	15,208	18,503
Dividend & Interest Income	15,510	16,635	17,380	20,508	37,476
Interest Exp—Existing Debt	(11,786)	(11,282)	(10,714)	(9,353)	(4,119)
Interest Exp—Redemption	(49,383)	(94,107)	(87,356)	(71,659)	15,567
Income before Income Taxes	107,086	54,318	147,487	112,421	465,139
Income Taxes	(28,280)	(10,456)	(45,268)	(30,523)	(173,497)
NET INCOME (LOSS)	$78,807	$43,862	$102,219	$81,898	$291,642

_____Dad's Manufacturing Company_____
Cash Flow Adjustments
(For the year ending December 31)

Projected future years

	Year 1	Year 2	Year 3	Year 5	Year 10
NET INCOME (LOSS)	$78,807	$43,862	$102,219	$81,898	$291,642
Add:					
Depreciation	58,200	58,200	58,200	58,200	58,200
Deduct:					
Capital Additions	(40,000)	(40,000)	(40,000)	(40,000)	40,000)
Principal Payments	(3,975)	(4,479)	(5,047)	(6,409)	(11,642)
Principal Payments —					
Stock Redemption	(29,907)	(64,474)	(71,225)	(86,922)	(143,014)
Cash flow	$63,125	($6,891)	$44,147	$6,767	$155,186
Beginning Cash	356,198	419,323	412,431	509,311	859,302
ENDING CASH	$419,323	$412,431	$456,578	$516,077	$1,014,488

CORPORATE CASH FLOW—NOTES AND ASSUMPTIONS

Sales. Sales for Year 1 have been projected based on results through May, Year 1. Future years' sales have been projected using the trend indicated, which is based on the past fifteen years' history.

Cost of Sales. Cost of sales has been projected at 68% of sales, based on the average of the prior three years.

Owners' Salaries. It is assumed that Dad's and Mom's salaries will no longer be paid after June, Year 1. Son No. 1's salary is assumed to increase to $50,000 in mid-Year 1 to reflect his increased responsibilities, and to grow by 4% per year thereafter. Son No. 2 and Daughter are assumed to receive raises for the first four years, and then to receive increases of 4% per year.

Consulting Agreements, Supplemental Pensions, and Noncompete Covenants. These agreements are reflected as paid as described in the overview.

Other Salaries. Salaries for Year 1 are projected by management, and are assumed to increase by 4% per year.

Payroll Taxes & Benefits. Payroll taxes and benefits are projected at 20% of total salaries, based on the average of the prior three years.

Profit-Sharing Plan. Qualified plan contributions are projected at 5% of total salaries.

Rents. Rents are projected at $4,900 per month under the existing lease, which calls for 5% per year increases.

Depreciation and Capital Additions. Depreciation expense assumes that all existing assets will be depreciated over the next seven years. New acquisitions are projected by management to cost $40,000 per year, of which $10,000 will be expensed using the Section 179 election and the remaining balance will be depreciated using the straight-line method over seven years.

Divided & Interest Income. Income is projected assuming a 4% per year return on the projected average cash balance.

Interest Expense and Principal Payments. The existing debt is being amortized over twelve remaining years at 12%, with monthly payments of $1,313.

The Redemption note is amortized over ten years at 10%, with monthly payments of $13,215 beginning July, Year 1 through June, Year 11.

Income Taxes. Federal income taxes are estimated using the current graduated corporate tax rates. State income taxes are projected at 5% of income before income taxes.

Other Income and Expenses. All other income and expenses, not otherwise mentioned above, are assumed to increase by 4% per year.

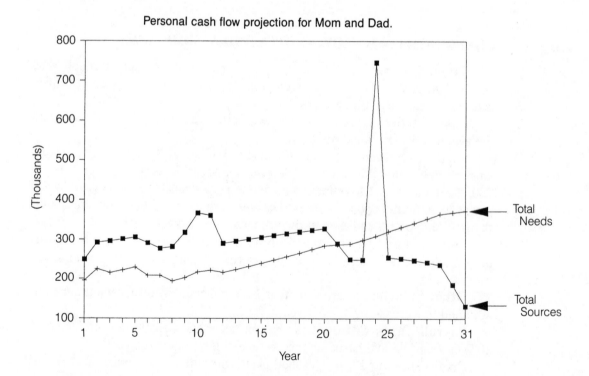

Personal cash flow projection for Mom and Dad.